A devotional for parents of extraordinary children

SOUL CRIES

By Theresa Regan

SOUL CRIES:
A devotional for parents of
extraordinary children

ISBN: 1478221615
ISBN-13: 9781478221616

Library of Congress Control Number: 2012912768
CreateSpace, North Charleston, SC

Author photo by Cindy Schultz, Shelby Studios Photography

The author can be contacted at soulcriesdevotional@gmail.com

THIS BOOK IS DEDICATED TO FAMILIES.

Ephesians 3:14-17 (New International Version)

For this reason I kneel before the Father, from whom every family in heaven and on earth derives its name. I pray that out of his glorious riches he may strengthen you with power through his Spirit in your inner being, so that Christ may dwell in your hearts through faith.

FOREWARD

I wondered whether I should go to the conference.

The radio station I manage was a finalist for an award at the Christian Music Broadcasters conference, so I felt responsible to represent the station. But it was a thousand miles from home. Our fourteen-year-old son was having an epic health struggle. The many doctor visits we had made to several different experts over the preceding twelve months had yielded no answers, and because of his ongoing special needs, my wife, Donna, and I were exhausted physically and emotionally.

I worried that if I went to the conference and Wes took a turn for the worse, it would be too much for Donna to bear alone. She felt that I should go. I was on the fence. She won.

On the second day of the conference, a text arrived. It was a distress message from home. The phone conversation that followed gave the rest of the story. It was not just a "bad day;" it was one of the worst in our entire saga.

With Donna depleted and sobbing, I felt helpless being so far from home. I stepped out of the conference session to pace the hallway; I beat myself up for making the trip, and I cried out to God inwardly. *Should I catch a plane and get home as soon as possible? How could I have put my wife in this position? God, can you please do what I can't? Please BE THERE for her and our son.*

Within the next fifteen minutes, something remarkable happened.

Heartsick, I headed to my room to check my email. This note had just arrived in my inbox:

Dave & Donna,

"In our prayers, it occurred to us that you and your family have a key position at the radio station and in the community. We are wondering if you have regular prayer covering, and feel like God would like us to cover your family in prayer. Pat and I commit to cover your family, household, health, finances, job, school, etc., in prayer from now until Christmas."

Blessings,
Pat and Theresa Regan

How does God do it? The precision of timing? The intricacy of detail?

We had met Pat and Theresa a couple of years earlier but did not know them well. They knew little of our situation with our son. The idea of praying for our family was not something we had ever discussed. It was by the Spirit.

That was a holy moment—alone in my hotel room. But suddenly I did not feel alone. I knew that Donna was not alone. God came near, and so did the Regans. Pat began recruiting other trusted prayer warriors to join in providing daily intercessory prayer for us. Theresa began sending emails each day to the group offering specific direction for prayer focus. **Operation Prayer Shield** was born.

Seventeen days after Theresa and Pat began offering daily prayer cover, we found the root cause of our son's mystifying health issues that had nearly taken his life. We began to see the unfolding of a miracle story right before our eyes.

The messages in this book come from the heart of a faithful and faith-filled woman of prayer who listens carefully as a part of her prayer experience. Time after time, over the past two years, Theresa's daily Operation Prayer Shield updates have focused on the exact passage of scripture that Donna and I have just read, or they have offered the same theme we've just felt the Holy Spirit whispering to our hearts.

As a mother and a medical professional, Theresa knows firsthand the challenges that families with struggling children face. Her message is not one of lofty theory. It has been formed in the crucible of daily reality. She offers fresh insights to help us skillfully wield the Sword of the Spirit as we contend for God's purposes to be fulfilled in and through our loved ones.

When you've experienced something remarkable firsthand, you want to share it with others. That's exactly how we feel.

Our prayer is that God will speak personally and powerfully as you read *Soul Cries*. May the Lord breathe LIFE into these meditations and give you hope, encouragement, and inspiration as His loving reminder that, although you may be in an incredibly hard place, you are not alone.

Dave Brooks
Station Manager
WCIC Radio

Donna J. Brooks, M.A.
Licensed Clinical Professional Counselor/Songwriter

Introduction

My name is Theresa. I was born in Michigan. When I was five, I learned to read and enjoyed playing make-believe with my sister. When I was seven, I took ice skating lessons. At ten, I got braces. My mother taught me to bake when I was eleven. By the time I was twelve, I was the oldest of five children.

In high school, I loved to sing. I met my husband as a sophomore when we performed in *Fiddler on the Roof* together. When I was seventeen, I told a friend that I would like to learn about the brain in college. I went to graduate school, took tennis lessons with my roommate, and enjoyed summer vacations at the Georgian Bay with my family. When I was twenty-eight years old, my parents walked me down the aisle, and I married my husband, Patrick.

At age thirty, my husband and I packed up all of our belongings and drove from Michigan to Illinois. We rented a duplex. We worked and studied. We enjoyed the coffee shop down the street. We bought our first home and mowed the lawn. When I was thirty-six, I experienced morning sickness and wore maternity clothes. At thirty-seven, I carried our son, Joshua, into our home for the first time.

In the years that followed, we learned about many new things. We were introduced to diapers and pacifiers, baby swings and strollers. We began to understand colic and food sensitivities. We became experts on Star Wars, pirates, and LEGOs. We were schooled on weighted blankets and sensory symptoms.

We also came to understand so much more about the autistic spectrum, with all its strengths and weaknesses, gifts and struggles.

Today, working in a hospital setting, I interact with many families facing the challenges of having a child with a physical illness or injury. I'm in a community with families who are trying to help their children overcome learning problems, tackle anxieties, and develop social and relational skills in difficult situations. I'm aware of the struggles that parents and children wrestle with, gain from, and often wrestle with again.

This book was born out of living, seeing, and knowing. It was written for anyone praying over the life of a child who struggles and faces challenges. I have seen your wrestling. I have seen the heart you have for your children. I pray that this book will declare God's goodness over your household and encourage you in your faith.

1

CONFIDENCE

1 JOHN 5:14-15 (AMPLIFIED BIBLE)

And this is the confidence (the assurance, the privilege of boldness) which we have in Him: {we are sure} that if we ask anything (make any request) according to His will (in agreement with His own plan), He listens to and hears us. And if (since) we {positively} know that He listens to us in whatever we ask, we also know {with settled and absolute knowledge} that we have {granted us as our present possessions} the requests made of Him.

This passage in First John talks about living in confidence and assurance as we pray, intercede, and request things from the good Father. We are called to do two things: to live in agreement with God, and to live with a positive knowing and trust that God listens and works on behalf of our intercessions.

We are to pray boldly and confidently in agreement with God. In all our thinking, planning, dreaming, resting, and working, we are to move and breathe in agreement with Him. We should have no thought about our circumstances or our future that God does not have. We should not make a home in our hearts for emotions that have no place in Him. Is God fearful? Is God shamed? Is God defeated? No. We are to live in agreement with everything that is part of Him, and we are to pray in this same spirit of agreement.

When we live and pray within this framework, we can positively know that He hears our soul cries. He knows the desires of our hearts. These cries agree with the heartbeat of heaven. We are then settled in a deep sense of knowing that lets us rest in Him—knowing that we have what we request. These soul cries for justice, rightness, and goodness are our possessions in Him. They are granted by the Father.

1. In what ways do you live in agreement with the Father? Is there anything about your thoughts, emotions, or prayers that is not in agreement with God's heart? Pray that God will reveal truths to your heart this week.

2. What are your soul cries? Do you cry out for your child, your family, your household? Cry out with a heart that beats with God, and live in a posture of assurance that God hears you, knows you, and grants your request.

2

Holy Plans

Jeremiah 1:5 (The Message)

Before I shaped you in the womb, I knew all about you.
Before you saw the light of day, I had holy plans for you...

In this passage, God is speaking to Jeremiah about his identity and destiny in Him. He tells Jeremiah that he has been known by God before he was even shaped in the womb. There was a holy plan over his life; he was called to be a prophet to the children of Israel. I believe that God's delight is the relationship He has with His creation. I believe He knows us intimately and individually, and that He speaks identity and destiny over each one of us. I do not think that anyone is here by chance, but rather by design.

Look at each of your children. God sees them and knows them. He speaks identity and significance over their lives. They are created to impact their world for good, and to partner with God to bring about brilliance and wonder. They are created to hear His voice and respond. They are called and sent. God has holy plans for each of them. Can you hear God's heartbeat over your children? Rejoice! They are called to change the world.

1. If you see your children struggling, you may feel concern about their future and their role in the world. Ask God to enlighten your heart about their God-given identity and destiny. They are called to fulfill a great purpose in God.

2. Have you heard God speak over your life? What is your identity and destiny? What is His holy plan for you?

3

Hunger and Thirst

Matthew 5:6 (New International Version)

Blessed are those who hunger and thirst for righteousness, for they will be filled.

Are you hungry? Are you thirsty? What do you long for? What do you run after and search for? Scripture says that when we hunger and thirst for God and His righteousness, we will be filled! I love the image of filling. That hunger and thirst we feel at a soul level, that empty ache, that yearning for more: it is all there because there is more—more, more, and more of God!

Fill us up, Lord; fill us to overflowing, and then fill us up even more! We welcome your Presence in our lives. We make room for you and prepare a place for you. We lay ourselves at your feet and soak you in.

When you are parenting a child who has specific needs, you may feel emptied out. I pray that you will know where to fill up again. I pray that your hunger for God will increase. I pray that you will be starving for more, thirsting for more, and that you will know how to satisfy your hunger in the very Presence of God. May you be filled, yet remain hungry to be filled some more.

1. Do you feel a hunger for God? If not, let's pray together that your appetite for God's Presence will increase as you spend time with Him. *God, I pray that you will make this son or this daughter ache for your Presence.*

2. Have you tried to fill yourself with something other than the Presence of God? Have you felt satisfied and filled? I pray that God Himself will fill you up!

4

SUDDENLY

LUKE 5:5-7 (THE MESSAGE)

Simon said, "Master, we've been fishing hard all night and haven't caught even a minnow. But if you say so, I'll let out the nets." It was no sooner said than done—a huge haul of fish, straining the nets past capacity. They waved to their partners in the other boat to come help them. They filled both boats, nearly swamping them with the catch.

When you are the parent of a child whose needs are complex and difficult, the days roll into months and years. The amount of effort can feel so tremendous compared to the amount of lasting gains. We may cry out to God, "We've been hard at it during this night season, and we haven't caught even a minnow!" When Simon says this to Jesus, he has good reason. Simon is an expert fisherman; he runs a business and knows when and where to catch fish. He has come back exhausted and empty-handed, but Jesus tells him to go out again and put the nets in the water one more time. It seems futile to Peter and the fishermen with him, because they have been out there all night trying so hard and have come back so very exhausted.

Yet, when the Master says it, they do it. They know Him and trust Him. His word means something true to them. They have that kind of relationship, and "it was no sooner said than done!" Suddenly there is a breakthrough where there had been no breakthrough. Suddenly there is supply where there had been no supply. Suddenly there is abundance where there had been lack. "Suddenly," after a long night of nothing, everything changed at the command of Jesus. Their "huge haul" of fish was surprising, abundant, and so heavy that it nearly sank the boats.

1. Beloved, have you been "fishing hard all night?" Have you done everything you know to do, but have come back exhausted and empty-handed? I pray that your heart will be open to unexpected wisdom from the Father. I pray that your hard night will turn "suddenly" into abundance and breakthrough!

2. How can you open your heart to hearing from God after such a long time of feeling empty-handed? In what ways can you strengthen your relationship with the Master so that you will go out and try again, trusting Him to be true to His Word?

5

Beloved

Song of Solomon 2:4 (Amplified Bible)

He brought me to the banqueting house, and his banner over me was love {for love waved as a protecting and comforting banner over my head when I was near him}.

What a beautiful image. God brings us to a banqueting house. We are brought into a celebration of feasting, and He covers us with His love! We are covered, warmed, and protected by the love of the Most High God. There are times when life feels more like a battle than a feast. Yet, we are invited to feast with the King, and we are protected and covered, but with what? With His love—with God's perfect, abundant, joyous love.

It is important that you know, down to your core, that you are the beloved. It is essential that you enter into the feasting and covering of God today. Be covered, be filled, and be loved. Let God's love warm and calm you today. Let it cover your children and your household. Say, "You love me so much, God!" Shout with joy as you declare, "My children are beloved of God!"

1. Do you live with a knowing that you and your children are the beloved of God, covered in His perfect love? What thoughts or feelings get in the way of owning this truth?

2. In what way can you enter into feasting with God today? How can He fill you up?

6

SIGNIFICANCE

JUDGES 6:11-12, 14-16 (CONTEMPORARY ENGLISH VERSION)

Gideon was nearby, threshing grain in a shallow pit, where he could not be seen by the Midianites. The angel appeared and spoke to Gideon, "The LORD is helping you, and you are a strong warrior"... Then the LORD himself said, "Gideon, you will be strong, because I am giving you the power to rescue Israel from the Midianites." Gideon replied, "But how can I rescue Israel? My clan is the weakest one in Manasseh, and everyone else in my family is more important than I am." "Gideon," the LORD answered," you can rescue Israel because I am going to help you!"

Don't you love a good story? Tell me a story, God. Tell me a good story. Gideon is a very good story! Picture Gideon threshing grain in a pit so that the enemy won't come and steal his harvest. He is hiding in this pit when an angel appears to him and calls him a warrior. Hail mighty warrior! Gideon explains, of course, that he is insignificant, small, and powerless against the mighty enemy. He is the most insignificant man in the weakest clan. However, God calls him a warrior and says, "I am giving you the power to rescue Israel" from the enemy. God was with him!

How do you view your significance...your strength...your power? What enemies do you and your family face? God will find you and call out your future. He will find you, even if you are hiding, and even if you have pronounced yourself insignificant. He will clothe you in His power to free those who are captives of the enemy. He will empower you to succeed in the battle that you are called to fight. Hail mighty warrior!

1. Is there a battle in your life that you feel unprepared to fight? What unexpected enemies are you facing today?

2. Have you explained to God why your contribution is insignificant? What has His response been?

7

Encounters

Luke 2:51
(The Message)

His mother held these things dearly, deep within herself.

In this scripture, Mary is described as soaking in all that she has heard and seen as she journeys with Joseph and Jesus through God's plan. She has encountered an angel, interacted with shepherds, and seen wise men kneel before her as she held her small son Jesus. She has encountered Simeon and Anna in the temple and heard their blessings and prophetic declarations about identity and destiny. She has watched and listened to it all. She has soaked it in and kept it all deep within her heart. She would need it all in coming years, when her son would be beaten and crucified, and the hopeful future she had expected would seem dead.

In this life, we are invited to have encounters with God. There is great wisdom in treasuring these encounters and being a good steward of them in our hearts and minds by writing them down and calling them to mind. Each encounter is a gift to us. We should treat them all as treasures, golden and shining jewels. When God sees that you can receive an encounter, word, or promise and be able to steward it, He sees that you can steward more. Can we hold on to a word or promise for years and years, even when our circumstances seem the opposite? Are we able to hold on, steward, and treasure things deep in our hearts? Mary knew the importance of holding on to treasures and not letting them drop to the floor when "normal" life returns.

1. What has God given you that you have been able to steward for years, deep in your heart?

2. Have you had encounters with God, received words of encouragement, or had experiences that need to be resurrected in your heart and mind? How can you bring them to mind again and carry them in your heart today?

8

Kindness

Acts 28:2 (Amplified Bible)

And the natives showed us unusual and remarkable kindness, for they kindled a fire and welcomed and received us all, since it had begun to rain and was cold.

This has been a week of emotional struggle in my life; perhaps the most difficult week I have endured in a long time. Some significant things have happened, and I feel the weight and coldness of loss this week. I find myself crying easily, grieving. In the midst of this, I was walking out of our local grocery store one day. There was a vendor present who exchanged kind words with me and encouraged me. As I continued walking to the car, I heard him encourage and compliment every person who walked in or out of the store. That exchange was important to me that day. For some reason, it lifted me up. Even more than enjoying a compliment, I felt encouraged because I had been SEEN by another. I felt utterly alone, so heavy and wrapped up in my own thoughts, and he saw me and lifted me up.

We don't have to be a pastor or have a national ministry organization to offer kindness to others. That vendor was going about his business that morning; he didn't preach to me, give me advice, or tell me about biblical principles. He saw me, and he lifted me up. I felt ministered to. I thought of the scripture from Acts where Paul describes how the rain had set in and things had become cold. He was shown "unusual and remarkable kindness" by the natives who built a fire and welcomed Paul and everyone with him to join them.

1. How can you minister kindness to others today? As you go about your daily activities, what practical steps can you take to lift others up and receive them?

2. Make a goal today to show kindness to one, five, or ten people today. Believe that your gestures will be like a warm, cozy fire to them—an extraordinary kindness in the midst of a cold rain.

9

Opposites

Isaiah 61:1-4 (New International Version)

The LORD has anointed me...to comfort all who mourn, and provide for those who grieve in Zion—to bestow on them a crown of beauty instead of ashes, the oil of joy instead of mourning, and a garment of praise instead of a spirit of despair. They will be called oaks of righteousness, a planting of the LORD for the display of his splendor. They will rebuild the ancient ruins and restore the places long devastated; they will renew the ruined cities that have been devastated for generations.

This scripture is prophetic of the coming Messiah. In Luke 4, Jesus read Isaiah chapter 61 in the synagogue, which is also when He proclaimed His mission publicly. Let's read these first few verses together. They are so striking. The Lord anoints Jesus to bring an opposite spirit to a situation steeped in darkness. He is to bring beauty instead of ashes; joy instead of mourning; praise instead of despair. God calls us to the same mission. When we see lack, we are to trust in the abundance of God. When we are surrounded by hatefulness, we are to act in a spirit of peace and honor. When we sense fear around us, we are to shout out the faithfulness of God. We are created to walk in the spirit of God's light and to oppose the spirit of darkness.

See what Isaiah says next. He says that when those who grieve are given beauty for ashes, joy for mourning, and praise for despair, they will be a living monument to the glory, splendor, and goodness of God. They will rebuild the ancient ruins and restore the places that have been devastated for generations. Those who were given joy instead of grief were restored, and in turn, they would restore the ruins around them, ruins that had been devastated for generations. The restored people would become the restorers.

1. In what way are you and your household a people who grieve? God comes to bring you beauty, joy, and praise. Declare this over your children and your household today.

2. When you experience the restoration of God, you become a restorer. In what ways have you been a restorer of devastation around you? How can you teach your children to live in a restoration spirit, clothed in the beauty, joy, and praise that God brings?

10

Lifted Eyes

Psalm 121:1-4 (New International Version)

I lift up my eyes to the mountains—where does my help come from? My help comes from the LORD, the Maker of heaven and earth. He will not let your foot slip—he who watches over you will not slumber; indeed, he who watches over Israel will neither slumber nor sleep.

Blessed are you when you lift your eyes to the heights for help. Blessed are you when you know where your help comes from. Your help comes from the Maker of the heavens and the earth, the Creator of the universe. He is the God who watches over you, never resting, and never shifting His gaze or falling asleep. He is attentive to your needs, never letting you slip. Lift your eyes to Him. Lift your gaze up to the mountains, and see the God whose eyes meet yours.

Let's pray over your child together. I pray that your son will come to know his Creator intimately, and that he will feel God's watchful gaze on him and know where to seek help. I pray that your daughter will know how to sing to the heavens a song of praise. I pray that she will know and be known by the Maker of heaven and earth. May you all experience God's loving, healing, and peace-giving gaze over your life.

1. Do you feel that God is attentive to your needs? In what ways have you experienced His watchfulness over your life? In what ways do you struggle with knowing that He sees you?

2. Pray Psalm 121 over your life today, and over the lives of your children. Invite God to open your eyes to His attentions and His love for you and your household.

11

Open Spaces

Romans 5:1-2 (The Message)

We throw open our doors to God and discover at the same moment that he has already thrown open his door to us. We find ourselves standing where we always hoped we might stand—out in the wide-open spaces of God's grace and glory, standing tall and shouting our praise.

When you are the parent of a child with extraordinary needs, life can feel small, constrained, and cramped. I remember listening to our neighbor describe how some friends of hers decided at the last minute to meet up in a large city a few hours away and spend the weekend at a water park with all their kids. They all had a great time, were able to get to know each other better, and felt refreshed from this weekend vacation.

I thought, *Wow. That is so far from anything in my experience right now.* In our household, spontaneity can be difficult to attain. Routine, structure, and planning usually take center stage. At times, I feel the constraint of this structure, and it feels rigid and small. At these times, I meditate on scriptures about God's plan for wide-open spaces. This is a nice word-study to do in the scriptures, as this theme is repeated several times. The above scripture is one that I meditate on..."We find ourselves standing where we always hoped we might stand—out in the wide-open spaces of God's grace and glory."

We open our doors to you God, and we know that someday the tight spaces of constraint will be no more. Someday we will have wide-open spaces where we will live surrounded and overcome by your glory. Give us freedom and open spaces, God!

1. In what ways does your current space feel small and cramped?

2. God is a God who opens up space for us. How has God provided room for you? In what ways are you still waiting for the spaces to open?

3. How can you meditate on His promises during seasons of waiting?

12

PROCESS AND JOURNEY

HEBREWS 11:13 (NEW INTERNATIONAL VERSION)

All these people were still living by faith when they died. They did not receive the things promised; they only saw them and welcomed them from a distance, admitting that they were foreigners and strangers on earth.

Promises are promises, and God's promises are true. He is incapable of being unfaithful to a promise. By His very nature, He is a covenant-making God, and He interacts with His people accordingly. Nothing will fall short. However, He is also an eternal God—a God of the big picture. He is a God of the ages, not just of the moment. His vision crosses over seasons and times. As we see in Hebrews, there are aspects of the promise that unfold over time, perhaps even after a lifetime. Some of the promises the ancients received foretold of things to come generations into the future.

This is the good news and the hard news. We would all like to see promises brought to fruition in an instant. But our God is a God of process and journey. Some of His promises to us unfold over years, decades, and generations. It is hard to wait for promises to come true; perhaps we may get to the end of our lives feeling that some things we glimpsed are still far away. However, we praise God, for He is faithful to the generations. The way

God works in your life is part of a life-giving process that unfolds for your children and all generations to come. They will reap the benefit of your intercession, your prayer, and your journey. There will be breakthroughs that you strive toward your whole life that your children will receive as an inheritance without toil.

Thank you, God. Thank you for giving gifts to our children and being faithful to the generations. Thank you that our journey makes a difference; the promise is ever unfolding.

1. Sometimes faith in God's promises means believing that breakthrough will come to a future generation. What breakthroughs are you believing for your children?

2. What have you received as an inheritance because of the faith of your ancestors? Was there someone in a past generation who was a pioneer in the Christian faith and gifted you in your spiritual journey? How can you do the same for your children?

13

Unseen Things

2 Corinthians 4:18 (New International Version)

So we fix our eyes not on what is seen, but on what is unseen, since what is seen is temporary, but what is unseen is eternal.

What is seen is temporary. What is seen is incomplete, and will eventually pass away. As we pray into our circumstances, we pray for change and breakthrough in the visible realm. Sometimes what is seen does not seem to be changing. The visible realm may seem stuck, or it may even seem to be going from bad to worse. Yet, we offer prayers of thanksgiving, faith, worship, and petition. We listen for God's direction and His wisdom. We speak His words into the seen and the unseen realms. Sometimes, we wait and wait on the Lord.

It takes faith. We must choose to believe that our prayers, godly choices, and acts of faith are making an impact in the unseen realm. We must believe, even without seeing—without proof of change or impact. We choose to believe that our good, loving God is working on our behalf. We choose to believe that He always works all things for the good (Romans 8:28). This is faith. We choose to fix our eyes, not on what is seen, but on what is unseen. What is seen is temporary. What is unseen is eternal.

1. In what ways does the seen feel more real than the unseen? How can you fix your eyes on the unseen?

2. What role does community play in helping you focus on unseen things?

14

Labor and Life

Isaiah 66:9 (New International Version)

Do I bring to the moment of birth and not give delivery?" says the LORD. "Do I close up the womb when I bring to delivery?" says your God.

I carry this scripture in my mind and heart. I have been in that place where I have been laboring and laboring, in a place of pain and pressure with so little relief, feeling that nothing new has broken through—no new life. Likened to the birthing process, it is labor without life; pain and pressure without breakthrough. This verse speaks of the God who will not bring you to the season of pain and pressure without bringing forth new life. The phase of transition will end in life, in breakthrough, in something new.

If you are raising a child with extraordinary needs of any kind, you may feel that you have given birth, but you do not have your child. You may feel that your child is trapped, absent, or not fully present: not fully able to live life, build relationships, learn, and grow. God says that He will not bring us to the point of delivery and then make us unable to have our children.

1. *God, I pray over this reader. I pray that this mother or father will know courage and strength through the laboring, and soon they will experience breakthrough and see life.*

Focus on God as you labor, and know that life will break through!

2. Join me in praying for children across the world. I pray for children who are trapped or absent, wounded or ill. We speak God's life over every child that their every need will be evident and met. I speak healing and peace over them, their families, and their caregivers. *We want our children back, God! Bring restoration! Bring life!*

15

Perfume

2 Corinthians 2:14-15 (Contemporary English Version)

God also helps us spread the knowledge about Christ everywhere and this knowledge is like the smell of perfume. In fact, God thinks of us as a perfume that brings Christ to everyone.

The knowledge of Christ is a sweet fragrance to those around us. We are created to be carriers of this sweet perfume. No matter what is going on around us, we are called to be a blessing to others. It is easy to wait until we feel anointed, generous, or positive to release Christ's sweet fragrance. However, the perfume does not depend on whether our lives are fixed or we feel well. Even during seasons of struggle and wrestling, our ultimate mission and ministry is to be a blessing to the nations and generations.

I pray, reader, that your relationship with Christ, your journey with God, and your faith will be a sweet fragrance to those around you. I pray that you will release this perfume as a blessing and gift to your children, your family, and your community. May others breathe in the sweet scent of Christ and be changed because of your life, your choices, and your faith. May your life—complete with joys and struggles—be released as a blessing to generations to come.

1. Can you release your life and your journey with God to be a blessing to others? In what ways is this easy or difficult to do?

2. How has the perfume from others' lives been a blessing to you? Who has released the scent of Christ over you and your children during the seasons of your journey?

16

VICTORY

PSALM 21:1-2 (NEW INTERNATIONAL VERSION)

The King rejoices in your strength, Lord. How great is his joy in the victories you give! You have granted him his heart's desire and have not withheld the request of his lips.

How many times a day do you think we are invited by the Adversary to feel inadequate and overcome? I once spoke with the father of a young girl with special needs who was in what seemed like an endless struggle. The whole household was impacted in significant ways. The father spent many nights on his knees weeping and praying to God for intervention and breakthrough. One day he said, "I never thought I would give everything I have to raise my daughter, and it wouldn't be enough."

Without God, we are each inadequate. Separated from Him, we are incomplete and undone. But when we are in communion with Him, we are more than adequate! He brings victory into every circumstance we face. Speak the truth of God's Word into your situation right now by reciting Psalm 21. Pray with me: *I rejoice in your strength, Lord. How great is my joy in the victories that you give! You will grant me my heart's desire and not withhold the request of my lips!*

I believe God knows your heart, hears your cries, and will bring victory into your situation!

1. How can you embrace God's strength today?

2. How have you seen God bring victory into your life in the past?

3. What does God's victory look like?

17

Remember

Psalm 143:4-5 (New International Version)

So my spirit grows faint within me; my heart within me is dismayed. I remember the days of long ago; I meditate on all your works and consider what your hands have done.

Hebrew poetry is somewhat rhythmic, in that the first part of a verse and the second part echo each other. The first part of verse 4, for example, talks about a faint spirit, and the second part echoes that sentiment by talking about a heart filed with dismay. Verse 5 answers verse 4 by talking about remembering the days of old and meditating on the works of God's hands.

What does this have to do with life? I believe the psalmist is illustrating that when our spirits grow faint and our hearts are dismayed, we should meditate on God's works and remember what He has done. God loves to tell His story again and again; He tells His story throughout scripture and throughout all of our lives. Have you recognized how God tells His story in your life? Have you had encounters with God at various times in your life? Have you experienced His redemption, peace, wisdom, or forgiveness?

God is revealed through the scriptures and through His hand at work in our life experiences. I have found it helpful to write about my experiences with God. Every now and then, I take out my journal and read through the years—my journey with God. I share these stories with my family members so that they will know what God has done in my life. When we feel faint-hearted, we must meditate on what God has done. This keeps us focused on Him instead of our circumstances or worries. It brings us into the truth and invites God to come and tell His story in our lives again and again!

1. What are your favorite stories from scripture? How do they reveal God's character and heart?

2. What are your own personal stories of how God has worked in your life? Keep a journal this year of moments that have been wrought by the hand of God. In writing them down, you will most likely discover that you have had more experiences with Him throughout your life's journey than you may have realized! Commit to reading your stories; it will keep your heart from being dismayed.

18

Homecoming

Zephaniah 3:18-20 (The Message)

"The accumulated sorrows of your exile will dissipate. I, your God, will get rid of them for you. You've carried those burdens long enough. At the same time, I'll get rid of all those who've made your life miserable. I'll heal the maimed; I'll bring home the homeless. In the very countries where they were hated they will be venerated. On Judgment Day I'll bring you back home—a great family gathering! You'll be famous and honored all over the world. You'll see it with your own eyes—all those painful partings turned into reunions!" God's Promise.

I like word pictures. The image of accumulated sorrows and carrying burdens is so vivid. I can easily resonate with the feeling of sorrows adding up and feeling heavy on your heart and soul. In Zephaniah, God says that the sorrows of your separation will dissipate. He promises to rid the people of the sorrow and of the enemies that have come against them and robbed them. He says He will heal their afflictions and bring them home. They will not be ashamed, despised, or looked down on. They will be held up as honored and favored. There will be restorations of relationships and a true homecoming.

This scripture emphasizes the restorative heart of God. It reveals His eternal plan for making things right again and again throughout history and across people groups. God loves to tell and retell the story of who He is. He wants to tell His story in your life and in the life of your child. He is a God of healing and restoration. He is a God who will take away your sorrows and burdens. He will bring you home and you will be honored and blessed. It is part of His character and part of His commitment to His people.

1. Are you carrying the weight of a heavy burden of sorrows? Pray with me: *Jesus, we pray that you will bring release and restoration into this household. We pray that you will come with your healing and gather your children to you.*

2. How can you entrust your heart to God today? Talk to Him about your sorrows and your desires for restoration. Share your heart with Him now.

19

No Room for Fear

Psalm 3:6
(New International Version)

I will not fear though tens of thousands assail me on every side.

Sometimes we find ourselves surrounded by enemies in this life—thousands of enemies, and enemies on every side. We may find ourselves surrounded by problems of health, finances, relationship betrayal, grief, and loss. We may see our children surrounded by enemies and feel helpless to protect them.

There is a difference between feeling afraid and actually making an internal home for fear. We can actually make a space in our lives for fear and say, "Yes, come in. I've prepared a room for you with a bed and chair. I've swept it clean and you can stay with me now." We can prepare a place for fear by the way we think, by focusing on fearful thoughts, and by agreeing with fearful speculations or declarations. We may be encouraging our children to invite fear in and make a place for it. This invitation and agreement is what God tells us not to do. Don't give fear space; don't agree with it or let it take root within you.

Rather, say with the Psalmist, "I will not fear though tens of thousands assail me on every side." The enemy exists and is numerous, but we must choose not to let fear get a foothold in our lives. Let each of us say, "I see the enemy, but I'm not impressed. My God is bigger and stronger. He protects me from every enemy and saves me!" Rather than declaring fear, let us declare the saving power of God and beckon Him to protect and defend us.

1. Can you think of a time when you made space for fear in your life by meditating on the enemy's numbers and strength? Have you felt fearful for your child, your finances, or your health?

2. What are some practical ways you can declare that you are not afraid of the enemy? How can you choose to focus on and meditate on God and His promises? How can you live in the belief that the big picture is filled with life, promise, and breakthrough?

20

Blessing

Genesis 12:1-3 (The Message)

God told Abram: "Leave your country, your family, and your father's home for a land that I will show you. I'll make you a great nation and bless you. I'll make you famous; you'll be a blessing. I'll bless those who bless you; those who curse you I'll curse. All the families of the Earth will be blessed through you."

Sometimes, life takes a curve, and you realize you are not in Kansas anymore. This is not your mother and father's land anymore, and it's nothing you recognize, either. How do you navigate those curves in your life, especially when they involve hardship and challenging situations that are not easily fixed? One thing I try to do is to get out of myself and turn my gaze outward. I meditate on this scripture and recite to myself, "You will be a blessing to others. Everyone on earth will be blessed because of you."

I am coming to understand that in good times and difficult situations we are called to be a blessing to everyone we encounter. More foundational than any individual mission or gifting we may have, we are all called to be a blessing to those around us. It helps me to come up for air from my own troubles by looking around me. I think one of the agendas of the Enemy is to keep us so distracted that we never minister to people near us. Whether consciously or subconsciously, sometimes we think we should wait until we gain victory in our lives before reaching out to help others. The enemy would love to keep us so busy, defeated, distracted, and tired that we never focus on our biggest mission: to be a blessing.

1. Identify one practical thing you can do today to bless someone near you.

2. How can you impact your family, church, city, and nation for good in an increasingly global and long-term way?

3. In what ways do you shut down when you are distracted and struggling? Are you waiting until things "settle down" before you minister to others?

21

Calm

Judges 6:24 (Contemporary English Version)

Gideon built an altar for worshiping the LORD and called it "The LORD Calms Our Fears."

As a parent, there are times and seasons when fear can take on an almost physical reality, as if we can feel the hand of fear take hold. The source of the fear in the natural may vary. For instance, we may worry about the choices we make or our ability to get through the day. We may worry about finances or how to get supportive services to meet our children's needs. But whatever the source, the spirit is the same. It is the spirit of fear.

In this scripture, Gideon has just had a personal, life-changing, supernatural encounter with God. He has received an impartation from God about his purpose and future. God says Gideon will set the people free from the oppression of the enemy. What did Gideon do in response to this experience? He built a monument—an altar for worshiping the Lord. He named the structure "The Lord Calms Our Fears!" He had a personal encounter with God. He understood who God was in a new way, a life-changing way. He met and encountered the Lord, who calmed His fears. Your God is not neutral or far away; He is for you, and He is so close. He is here to calm your fears.

1. Have you felt the grip of fear in your life? What do you fear?

2. The antidote to fear is to experience God personally. In His Presence, your fears will be calmed. How can you come into His Presence today?

22

ASSURANCE

ROMANS 8:28 (AMPLIFIED BIBLE)

We are assured and know that {God being a partner in their labor} all things work together and are {fitting into a plan} for good to and for those who love God and are called according to {His} design and purpose.

What do you feel sure of? What are the foundations of what you believe? What are the things that you never veer from, the beliefs from which everything else flows out of you? In Romans, Paul says that we can be assured that all things work together and are fitting into a plan for good. This is true for you. You can be sure of this and know it absolutely. You can build your home on this truth. You can raise your children on this foundation. You can set your marriage firmly in this verse. This is true for those who love God and are called to His purpose!

Sometimes I look at all the struggles around me. I see tragedy in history, in the world, and in my community. When something takes my breath away, I need to regroup. I say, "Wow, God's glory—His eternal goodness—must be so incredible if it can eclipse darkness like this. I am encouraged and blessed to have a God who can turn this horrible thing into His plan for good!" When you see something dark and grievous, meditate on how wonderful God's glory is that it can bring good out of something that dark. Nothing puts out the Light. The Light shines over all things. In the end, everything must work for good for those who love God and are called into purpose with Him through Christ!

1. When you see struggles around you, how can you fix your eyes on the promise that good will be the outcome?

2. What do you feel sure of? Do you build your household on the foundation of God's goodness?

23

Roots

Jeremiah 17:7-8 (New International Version)

But blessed is the one who trusts in the LORD, whose confidence is in him. They will be like a tree planted by the water that sends out its roots by the stream. It does not fear when heat comes; its leaves are always green. It has no worries in a year of drought and never fails to bear fruit.

Parenting a child requires wisdom, stamina, love, faith…oh, so many things. When your child has needs beyond the norm, the requirements to get through the day can feel weighty, and at times, impossible. This verse from Jeremiah speaks to us when we feel that we are in the year of drought—all dried up, hot and weary. It is amazing to meditate on the promises in this scripture.

Jeremiah 17 says that I am blessed when my trust and confidence is in the Lord. Why? Because my roots go deep into the supernatural stream of His refreshment and provision. I have no worries when I am filled up with Him. I won't fade away, fall apart, or dry up. The drought won't touch me, because my wellspring is deep within Him. I don't rely on the rain of the season.

Let me pray this scripture over you: *I pray that your confident, expectant trust in God will root itself into His deep streams of refreshment. I pray for you during the night, that you will know rest and refreshment. I pray for you in your daily activities, that God will provide you with all you need to "be green" and fruitful!*

1. When you feel dry and weary, focus on God's faithfulness. Pray for the streams of His refreshment to sustain you in the deep places of your heart.

2. When you are in a season of drought, you may need someone else to pray the scriptures over you, to speak truth into your life. Think of someone who can pray into your circumstances with scriptural truths, and tell that person how much his or her prayers help to sustain you.

24

FAITH

JEREMIAH 32:13-15 (THE MESSAGE)

Then, in front of all of them, I told Baruch, "These are orders from God-of-the-Angel-Armies, the God of Israel: Take these documents—both the sealed and the open deeds—and put them for safekeeping in a pottery jar. For God-of-the-Angel-Armies, the God of Israel, says, 'Life is going to return to normal. Homes and fields and vineyards are again going to be bought in this country'."

In this chapter, Jeremiah has prophesied, "This is what the LORD says: 'I am about to give this city into the hands of the king of Babylon, and he will capture it'." Jeremiah saw in the spirit that the enemy would come and conquer the land; the enemy would lead the Jewish people away to exile and captivity. In the midst of this vision of a conquered land, he also heard God tell him to buy a plot of that land from his cousin. So, he bought his cousin's land because he heard God saying that, in time, "Life is going to return to normal. Homes and fields and vineyards are again going to be bought in this country."

Jeremiah's act of buying the land was an act of faith, an investment in the future. Even though the land would slip away, he would own a portion of the future. He was saying yes to God's declaration that the people would return and own the land again. When you are parenting a child who faces daily challenges, you may relate to the feelings of loss or exile that the Jewish people lived through. The thought of "life returning to normal" may feel far off. You may feel you are living in a place of exile, a tremendous distance from the land that was taken. Living from a place of faith means that we live with belief for the future, relying on God's promises for our children, our household, and ourselves.

1. In what ways have you felt that your land and home have been taken by the Enemy? Have you felt in exile?

2. God told Jeremiah to buy land because "life is going to return to normal. Homes and fields and vineyards are again going to be bought in this country." How can you live in faith for the future? Does belief in a good future propel you forward?

25

Possibilities

Matthew 19:26 (New International Version)

Jesus looked at them and said, "With man this is impossible, but with God all things are possible."

Our foundational beliefs about life, God, and the future are so important. These beliefs shape how we approach life and how we posture ourselves in prayer. They are at the root of our attitudes and expectations. We teach our children, both deliberately and without realizing what we're doing, how to approach the expected and the unexpected, the now and the not yet, the fixed and the unfixed. This scripture speaks to one of the foundations of belief that sets in motion many other things. It talks about possibilities and what we believe God for.

With God, ALL things are possible. Do you believe this? Is your belief theoretical or is it practical and applicable for the real world? Do you live this belief? Do you own this belief deep in your heart and at the core of your being? All things are possible with God. Believe for more. Believe for breakthrough. Believe for things that are "impossible with man." I encourage you to approach each day believing that the impossible is possible!

1. Choose one thing in your life or the life of your child that you feel is impossible. Pray this scripture over that area of your life this month. Journal what God speaks to you as you pray, watch, and wait patiently for Him.

2. I pray over you right now, reader. I pray that supernatural faith will invade your heart and give you courage to believe for the impossible.

26

Not Alone

1 Kings 19:13-14, 18 (The Message)

When Elijah heard the quiet voice, he muffled his face with his great cloak, went to the mouth of the cave, and stood there.

(God) A quiet voice asked, "So Elijah, now tell me, what are you doing here?"

Elijah said it again, "I've been working my heart out for God, the God-of-the-Angel-Armies, because the people of Israel have abandoned your covenant, destroyed your places of worship, and murdered your prophets. I'm the only one left, and now they're trying to kill me." …

(God) Meanwhile, I'm preserving for myself seven thousand souls: the knees that haven't bowed to the god Baal, the mouths that haven't kissed his image."

Raising a child with specific needs can be isolating for so many reasons. You may be using all of your energy to find solutions, to problem-solve, and to make things better. You and your spouse may alternate responsibilities, or you may be a single parent, juggling everything on your own. Your resources may be drained. You may feel you are fighting a battle to set your child free, and you are not sure if you are winning.

Elijah felt the same way in the scripture above. He had just won a huge victory against four hundred fifty prophets of Baal. On top of that, a three-year drought was ended in a mighty way. But soon after these victories, he was exhausted from the fight and scared of the enemy. He explained to God how hard the fight had been and how little progress he felt had been made. He felt isolated, like the only one left who was fighting the good fight. He said, "I'm the only one left, and now they are trying to kill me." He was exhausted, isolated, and drained…not sure of any progress. But God speaks the truth over his situation. God says that there are seven thousand others who are faithful to The Almighty who have not bowed to other gods. Those others were fighting the good fight too.

You are not alone. You are not the only one fighting the good fight for your children. We join you in prayer for breakthrough, for victory, for strength, and for courage. I know the cries of your heart, and I tell you that you are not alone. I pray that friends and community will surround you in practical ways every day.

1. Have you felt isolated in your struggle to help your child? How can you become more integrated with others who share your battle and heart?

2. God sees you and knows you. How can you embrace God's heart for you today?

27

Vision

Proverbs 29:18 (The Message)

If people can't see what God is doing, they stumble all over themselves; But when they attend to what he reveals, they are most blessed.

I am constantly learning new things about God, adjusting my perspective, and growing in a deeper knowledge of Him. One of the things I am realizing as I continue my journey with God is that the way to get through a hard time is to have God's vision for the future. Although there is a place for processing the past and problem solving the present, the power of the future that God sees and promises is compelling. It gives us the momentum to move forward. What keeps us going is God's revelation of the big picture, His promises for the future, and His speaking of destiny and purpose over our household.

Pray with me: *God, we pray for vision and seeing. We ask for revelation about what you are doing, seeing, and speaking. Give us your perspective, your eternal vision for the big picture. Bring us out of our present moment and sustain us with your revelation of purpose, promise, and restoration. Give us vision for the future, vision that propels us forward through difficult seasons.*

1. Do you have God's vision for your future and the future of your children? Pray that God will reveal the big picture to you.

2. Consider today how you can keep your eyes on God and keep moving forward in His purpose and plan. Journal about your thoughts.

28

CALLING

EXODUS 3:10-12 (NEW INTERNATIONAL VERSION)

So now, go. I am sending you to Pharaoh to bring my people the Israelites out of Egypt. But Moses said to God, "Who am I that I should go to Pharaoh and bring the Israelites out of Egypt?" And God said, "I will be with you..."

In this passage, Moses turns aside from shepherding his father-in-law's flock when he sees the burning bush that is not consumed by the fire. As he turns aside from his usual activities, God begins speaking to him about his identity and destiny as part of God's plan to free His people. God has a plan and purpose for this man who left Egypt forty years ago and does not even own the flock he is shepherding.

Moses feels inadequate to the task and asks, "Who am I...?" This is a familiar response to God's calling, isn't it? Can you recall any story in scripture in which God approaches someone and tells him/her of his/her identity and destiny, and that person responds by saying, "Oh yes! I can see why you would call me to do that. I am naturally gifted in that area and have extensive training. It makes perfect sense that you would choose me!" I can't. I recall people in the Bible explaining to God that they were too young, too old, slow of speech, cowardly, or barren. The list goes on, doesn't it?

Perhaps the correct question is not, "Who am I?" Perhaps the correct question is, "Who are you, God?" He is the God Almighty who makes creation out of the void, who calls things that are not as though they are. He is "I AM WHO I AM." He is everything. When Moses says, "Who am I?" God says, "I will be with you." That's the answer. Your identity and purpose is always found in and through God. I believe He speaks over you and calls you into great adventures with Him!

When you hear His call, say, "I know who you are, God. I don't have natural gifting to do that, and I feel untrained and inadequate, but, if you say it, God, it is true! May it be accomplished as you say because of who YOU are. And I know that you are with me!"

1. Have you sensed God calling you into something outside of your comfort zone? Have you ever felt inadequate to the task God has called you to accomplish?

2. In what ways has God taken you beyond yourself and into something bigger? Do you also believe He will do that for your child?

29

Rescue

Zechariah 9:11-12 (Contemporary English Version)

When I made a sacred agreement with you, my people, we sealed it with blood. Now some of you are captives in waterless pits, but I will come to your rescue and offer you hope. Return to your fortress, because today I will reward you with twice what you had.

God is in covenant with His people. He has made a sacred agreement with us, sealed with His blood. He is a promise-making and promise-keeping God. He sees you. He knows your children. He calls out to you when you are in the waterless pit. He understands your captivity and small spaces—your restricted room and your dark season. He is coming to your rescue. He is coming to you and your children to fill your lives with His living, eternal hope. The hope He gives will flow through you and your children like a river for generations to come.

Return to your fortress, the fortress of your God! He is bringing your reward. He is bringing restoration with twice what you lost. In the end, there is no loss in Christ, only gain. Your God is a God of restoration, flowing over, filled with hope, and lacking in nothing. Your household will not be empty, but rather filled to overflowing with double your loss. You and your children will know the restoring power of God, completely and eternally.

1. Talk to God about your captivity and loss. What are your struggles? What are your child's difficulties?

2. What in your life needs to be restored? What would hope feel like?

30

Fruitfulness

Galatians 4:27-28 (New International Version)

For it is written: "Be glad, barren woman, you who never bore a child; shout for joy and cry aloud, you who were never in labor; because more are the children of the desolate woman than of her who has a husband." Now you, brothers and sisters, like Isaac, are children of promise.

This can be a confusing passage, but it is an important one. Here, Paul is quoting Isaiah 54:1. This passage is not talking about whether it is a blessing to have children. That is already established in God's Word (Psalm 127:3-5). This scripture is talking about the greater theme of fruitfulness. Some things in our lives can be accomplished and brought about simply through human effort and determination. However, there are other things that we are unable to produce, fix, or accomplish. It is for these things that we must depend on God and His goodness, wisdom, promises, and faithfulness.

I believe that as humans, we all must face things that we cannot accomplish through our own efforts. For parents of children who are have specific needs, you may be faced daily with multiple things you wish you could change, fix, or make easier. The scripture in Galatians contrasts the barren woman, who is fruitful only through God's promise, with the married woman, who is able to bring forth children through natural means. It challenges us to rejoice and be glad when we are barren in certain areas of our lives, because that is when we are at the end of our abilities and we fall on our face before God; that is when we are able to have encounters with God. We are able to see His fruitfulness in our barren places. God produces more fruit in our lives, our circumstances, and our families than we ever could!

1. In what circumstances do you feel you are at the end of your abilities? Rejoice and prepare to meet God in that very situation! An encounter with God produces more fruit than your own striving ever will.

2. What Bible stories highlight God's interventions and fruitfulness in the lives of people who were unable to accomplish change through their own efforts?

3. Ask God today to invade areas of barrenness in your life. Keep a journal of what happens next!

31

Good News

Proverbs 15:30 (New International Version)

Light in a messenger's eyes brings joy to the heart, and good news gives health to the bones.

Sometimes it is easy to feed on bad news. Bad news travels quickly through the Internet, on the television, in the newspapers, and by word of mouth. We are deluged with worrisome thoughts. What if this happens? What if that happens? What will we do then? "They" say this, and "they" say that. Sometimes we excuse ourselves by saying that this focus on the negative is simply being realistic. We say we don't want to live with our "head in the clouds." But believe me, there is nothing more real than what God is doing, and what He is doing is always good. As Christians, we are called to live with our heads and minds in the cloud of His glory.

This verse from Proverbs emphasizes the importance of good news. The word "gospel" actually means "good news" or "glad tidings." As Believers, we are called to feed on the good news of what God is thinking, planning, and doing in our world. Why? This focus brings us into the truth, fosters our intimacy with God, and allows us to partner with Him in every circumstance. Meditating on the good news of Christ is an expression of our faith—faith that knows God's goodness is truer and more real than any bad event or worry we may experience. Scripture says that an awareness of the good news of God will bring fruit in every area of our lives.

1. I have friends who begin every business meeting with a discussion of good news. What practical steps can you take to focus on good news every day?

2. Is there an area in your life (your children, health, finances) that most tempts you to worry and focus on bad news? How can you foster faith and trust in this area?

32

One

John 17:20-23 (The Message)

I'm praying not only for them but also for those who will believe in me because of them and their witness about me. The goal is for all of them to become one heart and mind— Just as you, Father, are in me and I in you, so they might be one heart and mind with us. Then the world might believe that you, in fact, sent me. The same glory you gave me, I gave them, so they'll be as unified and together as we are—I in them and you in me. Then they'll be mature in this oneness, and give the godless world evidence that you've sent me and loved them in the same way you've loved me.

For those of you who are married or have been married, you know how very difficult it can be to sustain that close covenant relationship. Relationships do not often resemble greeting cards when you live day-in and day-out with someone, walking on the journey that life brings, going through seasons of struggle. I have read estimates that couples raising a child with extraordinary needs have a divorce rate near 85 percent. The fatigue and deep tiredness, and the uncertainty and strain can build and build. Your life may be in survival mode for so long that you may not even be able to pinpoint any specific moment when you and your spouse began to grow apart.

Today, let's join in prayer for marriages. We pray that marriages will not only survive, but will thrive. I pray that couples will know what it is to become one heart and mind, supernaturally, through God's Spirit. I pray that parents of children with specific needs will know such deep intimacy with God that they will grow in unity together. I pray they will know that they are filled with the same glory that filled Jesus, and that they will feel filled with that glory day after day and year after year. I pray, God, that they will know a life-giving oneness, a unity that sustains them in every season. May there be a kitting together of mind, body, and spirit. I pray that couples will know a supernatural resting in each other and in God. May there be no division, tension, or separating...but rather community and oneness.

1. I pray, reader, that you will have a deep intimate relationship that is filled with God's Spirit. May you know blessing, oneness, and the joy of a covenant relationship with Him.

2. If you are married, how can you breathe life into your marriage relationship today? If you are a single parent, I pray that God will send you an intimate partner to covenant with. May you know abounding blessings within a partnering relationship.

33

CREATION

GENESIS 1:2-3 (AMPLIFIED BIBLE)

The earth was without form and an empty waste, and darkness was upon the face of the very great deep. The Spirit of God was moving (hovering, brooding) over the face of the waters. And God said, Let there be light; and there was light.

In the lives of children with challenges, there are treatment decisions, financial obstacles, and the demands of communicating clearly to several different people about your child's ever-changing situation. There are times when you may feel emptiness and chaos, as if there is a void where wisdom and light should be. But when you invite the Spirit of God in, He moves, broods, and hovers. He broods over the darkness, the void, and the chaos until there is creation. He turns chaos into creation! God speaks, and there is light. The empty waste is replaced with beauty, wonder, creation, and life.

God, we invite you in to brood and create, and to bring light into our chaotic darkness. We invite you to create goodness out of chaos and nothing. We pray for light to shine into the darkness and penetrate it with clarity, knowing, and wisdom. We need vision, God. We need to see what you see and know what you know—an enduring vision rooted in our household, our minds, our bodies, and our circumstances. Come, God. Bring creation and light!

1. In what way does your child's functioning and treatment feel chaotic and void?

2. Invite the Holy Spirit to brood over the situation today. Let's pray for creation out of chaos, light out of darkness, and it will be good.

34

SPIRIT

2 TIMOTHY 1:7 (AMPLIFIED BIBLE)

For God did not give us a spirit of timidity (of cowardice, of craven and cringing and fawning fear), but {He has given us a spirit} of power and of love and of a calm and well-balanced mind and discipline and self-control.

When we ask God to enter our lives, He comes and abides in us. We become the living temple of God; His very Spirit lives in us. But the Spirit we are given is not the spirit of fear. You may have felt the spirit of fear surround you and ask to make a home in you. The problem is that the spirit of fear robs us of the gifts God's Spirit gives us. Fear takes away our power and leaves us cowering and hiding, and we gradually become smaller and smaller. We begin taking up less and less space in the world; we become invisible and isolated. Fear takes away our ability to love well. We become concerned with holding on to what we have, with maintaining the status quo, and with protecting our portion. We become unable to extend beyond ourselves, to give generously, to honor others, to covenant in relationships, and give to the community. Fear leaves us thinking of ourselves rather than others. Fear takes away our peace of mind, our groundedness, and our security in Christ. We are left drifting in the waves, our minds filled with "what ifs" and "oh, nos."

God's Spirit gives us power: power to stand and to move, and power to proclaim freedom to prisoners, to speak healing to the sick, and to declare life over the dead places. God's Spirit gives us the ability to love well, to love abundantly, flowing over, unceasing. God's Spirit brings deep peace and rest to our minds. When our thoughts agree with God's thoughts, we know unity and intimacy with God.

1. Have you felt the spirit of fear? Have you given it a place to live within you? How has fear reduced the abundance that you are meant to experience in God?

2. How can you say no to fear every day? What practical steps can you take to live without fear, but instead with power, love, and peace of mind?

35

GOD'S LOVE

EPHESIANS 3:16-17 (CONTEMPORARY ENGLISH VERSION)

God is wonderful and glorious. I pray that his Spirit will make you become strong followers and that Christ will live in your hearts because of your faith. Stand firm and be deeply rooted in his love.

When you invite God into your life, He comes and abides in you. You are His home and His temple. His very Spirit is present within you. He comes with glory and abundance to empower you with strength in Him. Then, your roots grow down, deep and full in His love. Yes, you become rooted and grounded in His love for you. That is where your security lies; that is your groundedness, your centering, your substance. It is in His love for you, your spouse, and your children.

This rooting is such a basic need for surviving and thriving as a parent, isn't it? Circumstances may come and go, but the roots are key because they are the foundation of everything. Read from Ephesians 3 aloud. Claim it for yourself and your children, for it is an eternal truth. When your roots are deep in His love, they will keep you strong. Rooting and grounding in anything else is sand and waves, tossing and turning. Be empowered with inner strength and trust in Him!

1. How deep do your roots go into God's love for you and your family? Where else have your roots attempted to find substance?

2. In what ways do you understand and know that God's Spirit makes His home in you? How has that impacted your life?

36

Fasting

Ezra 8:21 (New International Version)

There, by the Ahava Canal, I proclaimed a fast, so that we might humble ourselves before our God and ask him for a safe journey for us and our children, with all our possessions.

In this passage, Ezra has assembled a group of Jewish people to return to Jerusalem from their Babylonian captivity. Before the journey, he proclaimed a fast. He prayed for a safe journey for the Jewish people, for their children, and all their possessions. We are all on a journey, aren't we? Sometimes the journey feels like a big undertaking, filled with unknowns and twisting, turning paths. When we are leading our children on the journey, we are keenly aware of our need for Divine protection for safe passage.

As part of his prayer for safe passage for the Jewish people and their children, Ezra proclaims a fast. Have you ever combined fasting with prayer? There is a spiritual power in the discipline of fasting. There are many different ways to fast. When some people fast, they go without food, drinking only water. Others may fast from meat or some special type of food, such as sweets. Still others may fast from things such as computer/Internet time, video games, or television. You may be fasting alone or as part of a corporate fast (i.e., a group of people fasting together). There have been times when my family has fasted together despite being in different geographical locations. We have also participated in fasts with our church body. Fasting has always been a powerful way of coming before the Lord and praying for our families, our journey, and our destination.

1. What spiritual disciplines help you come before the Lord as you pray?

2. Have you ever combined fasting with prayer? What was your experience?

3. Consider fasting for a season, individually or corporately, as you pray for breakthrough in your family, community, or nation. I invite you to journal about your experiences during this season.

37

IDENTITY

MATTHEW 16:15-18 (THE MESSAGE)

He (Jesus) pressed them, "And how about you? Who do you say I am?" Simon Peter said, "You're the Christ, the Messiah, the Son of the living God." Jesus came back, "God bless you, Simon, son of Jonah! You didn't get that answer out of books or from teachers. My Father in heaven, God himself, let you in on this secret of who I really am. And now I'm going to tell you who you are, really are. You are Peter, a rock. This is the rock on which I will put together my church, a church so expansive with energy that not even the gates of hell will be able to keep it out.

In my experience, issues of identity are central. A large part of our life journey is spent figuring out who we are. Our perceived identity impacts our thinking, behavior, and relationships. I believe that the more we come to know God and enter into the truth about His identity, the more we come to know our own identity. Repeatedly in scripture, we see God speaking to people by name. Sometimes He changes a person's name as He brings out his or her full identity. Here, Jesus says, "I'm going to tell you (Peter) who you are, really are." I believe God calls out each person's identity. He is calling out your identity and that of your child, spouse, friend, neighbor, boss, and mechanic.

One issue that parents can struggle with is how to identify and describe their child's needs without "labeling" the child with an identity equal to a "disorder." This is a topic of hot debate, and I understand there are many arguments and positions. I will share some of my thoughts and where my heart is on this topic. I believe that God calls out a child's identity, and this identity is the central thing. It is separate from any other "label." However, diagnoses can be a place to start as far as communicating needs to clinical staff or family members and accessing services that each child may need to thrive. Another task for parents is to teach their child how to recognize some of their challenges and gifts, and to be able to "wrap words" around these things for their own understanding, and for others. This can also be an opportunity to teach your child about individual differences, and to help him or her reach out to others who may be challenged in some way, too. The process of using words to describe their own strengths and challenges while remaining rooted and grounded in their Christ-spoken identity provides an important and life-giving balance for children.

1. What has God spoken to you about your identity? What about the identity of your child or others close to you?

2. How have you helped your child discover his or her individual identity while accessing services for needs and communicating with others about your child's strengths and challenges?

38

Always

Philippians 1:3-6 (New International Version)

I thank my God every time I remember you. In all my prayers for all of you, I always pray with joy because of your partnership in the gospel from the first day until now, being confident of this, that he who began a good work in you will carry it on to completion until the day of Christ Jesus.

I love Paul's message here to the Philippians. He lets them know that he is thinking of them constantly. They are in his heart and mind as he lives from day to day. His thoughts and prayers are with them and for them. He thinks of them with thankfulness, and he prays for them with joy. I want to commit to this mindset, as described by Paul, even in the midst of difficulty, obstacles, and darkness. I want my thoughts to be filled with thankfulness and my prayers filled with joy—always!

Paul continues to explain that he is confident. How can he be confident as he writes from a prison cell? Because his beliefs are rooted in his Almighty God, not in his circumstances. He writes of his confidence that the "good work" God has started in His people will be carried to completion until we see Jesus face to face. Every work that God does within you is for good. Be confident that each good work will continue to completion.

Nothing will be incomplete, undone, or lacking. Every good work will continue to completion!

1. How often do you find yourself thinking with thankfulness and praying with joy? What other ways do you catch yourself thinking and praying? What is the fruit of each approach?

2. What good works has God started in you and your children? Can you live with the confident understanding that every work will continue to fruition and completion until Jesus returns?

39

COVERED IN GLORY

HABAKKUK 2:14 (AMPLIFIED BIBLE)

But {the time is coming when} the earth shall be filled with the knowledge of the glory of the Lord as the waters cover the sea.

The glory of God shall cover the whole earth—His goodness will spread everywhere and cover all. There will be nothing uncovered by the knowing of His glory and goodness. We will all know the glory of God, and the earth shall be filled with it. The earth itself will be covered with the knowing of God's goodness.

I pray for each person in your household. I pray for a covering over you as the waters cover the sea. May you be overshadowed with the knowing, with the glory, and with the goodness of the Lord. May God's glory and goodness be the most real thing in your day. I pray that your knowledge of the glory will increase, glory to glory, goodness to goodness, a covering always.

1. Make plans to soak in the glory and goodness of God today.

2. What spirit covers you and your household from the heat of the day? How can you invite God to cover you as the waters cover the sea?

40

Resurrection

Ezekiel 37:1-6 (Contemporary English Version)

Some time later, I felt the LORD's power take control of me, and his Spirit carried me to a valley full of bones. The LORD showed me all around, and everywhere I looked I saw bones that were dried out. He said, "Ezekiel, son of man, can these bones come back to life?" I replied, "LORD God, only you can answer that." He then told me to say: Dry bones, listen to what the LORD is saying to you, "I, the LORD God, will put breath in you, and once again you will live. I will wrap you with muscles and skin and breathe life into you. Then you will know that I am the LORD."

You may be familiar with the story of Ezekiel and the dry bones. Ezekiel is standing in a valley that is filled with bones, and they are very white and very dry; in other words, they were very dead. There was no life within them. God asked Ezekiel, "Can these bones come back to life?" God then instructs Ezekiel to speak to the bones by saying what God is saying. When you read the whole story (verses 1-14), you discover that Ezekiel speaks to the bones and they come to life and stand up. God explains that the dry bones are the people of Israel who feel dried up, with no hope for the future. God tells Ezekiel to tell the people, "I, the LORD God, promise to open your graves and set you free."

This is a wonderful story in many ways, and several themes could be developed and discussed from the story, but I ask that you meditate on two of them today. First, the answer to "can these bones come back to life?" is Yes! God establishes His character throughout scripture as one who restores, heals, builds, and resurrects. No bones are too dry, no hope too lost, and no pit too deep for Him to invade and restore.

Second, God did not come into that valley and tell Ezekiel to stand back and watch what He was about to do. He invited Ezekiel to speak the word of the Lord over the bones. God had intent and desire to resurrect the bones, and Ezekiel was called to speak God's resurrection over the bones. There was a partnering in that event, a role for Ezekiel, not to stand back, but to speak out. Ezekiel did not raise the bones; God's words did. But Ezekiel spoke God's words over a desolate valley! God then told him to speak His words of life over a people who felt dried up, worn out, and without hope.

There is a role for us in the resurrection process. We are called to hear what God is saying and to speak His words over the desolate valleys. We can speak life, hope, and resurrection over the lives of individuals and communities.

1. In what way do you feel dried up and without hope? Are there people in your life who can speak God's Word over you?

2. What situations around you are like the valley of dry bones? How can you speak God's Word and resurrection into those situations?

3. How might Ezekiel's model of speaking over dry bones inspire you to take a new approach to prayer and intercession?

41

Master Builder

Psalm 118:21-25 (The Message)

Thank you for responding to me; you've truly become my salvation! The stone the masons discarded as flawed is now the capstone! This is God's work. We rub our eyes—we can hardly believe it! This is the very day God acted— let's celebrate and be festive! Salvation now, God. Salvation now! Oh yes, God—a free and full life!

I praise you, God! What a wonderful God we have. His thoughts and plans are so different from our own. There was once a stone that others determined to be worthless. It was a stone rejected as flawed and cast aside by human builders. But God determined it to be the most important stone of all; it became the capstone, the foundational stone, of everything else. What victory, what surprise, what happiness! God takes what others see as worthless and builds a mighty tower. He sees destiny, purpose, and value in what others have cast aside; He is a master creator and builder!

1. God sees worth in things that humans reject and cast aside. Is there anything in your life or the life of your child that has been

determined worthless? How does God call value out of that area or situation?

2. What testimonies have you seen and heard from people who were considered useless, having no discernible gifts or contributions, only to rise up and change their communities and world?

42

Rejoice

Romans 12:15 (New International Version)

Rejoice with those who rejoice; mourn with those who mourn.

I believe this scriptural principle is key to being like Christ. It has also been one of the most difficult things for me to put into practice. I find the second part, mourning with those who mourn, easier than the first part. Rejoice with those who rejoice! This means that when I am mourning something in my own life, praying for breakthrough and wrestling with something difficult, I am called to rejoice with someone who already has what I am praying for. Let's say I have lost my job and am praying for a new one. One of my friends calls very excited because she has just been given a promotion and a raise! "Isn't God good?!" she says. Can I rejoice with her?

This scripture really challenges me. My family needs breakthrough in many areas: We need prayers answered! It can feel like many other families have attained the things we need without effort. So I can honestly say that this is one of the most powerful scriptural principles I have ever committed myself to. When I say that I am so happy that their household and kids are doing well and that I wish them every blessing (even ones that I am still contending for), I feel the Spirit of God present in a powerful way. I really do!

1. In what ways are you mourning? Who mourns with you?

2. How do you feel when others are rejoicing about a breakthrough in an area you are still struggling with? How can you commit to rejoice with them? Ask God to give you wisdom and strength in this area.

43

On Earth

Matthew 6:9-10 (New International Version)

This, then, is how you should pray: Our Father in heaven, hallowed be your name, your kingdom come, your will be done, on earth as it is in heaven.

How should we pray? Have you ever felt at a loss as you pray? If you have children who are struggling, you may pray and pray, only to feel more lost. Your words may feel spent and your direction and purpose blurred. In this scripture, Jesus is teaching His followers how to pray, and He gives them what we now call the Lord's Prayer. The first portion of the prayer gives me such grounding. In every situation, I know I can pray "Your Kingdom come, your will be done, on earth as it is in heaven."! Repeat it with me: on earth as it is in heaven. Pray it in the morning, in the noontime, and in the evening. Speak it over your children, your spouse, and yourself: on earth as it is in heaven!

I pray over your home right now, reader. May your home and family know God's Kingdom come to earth. I pray that God's divine desires will be accomplished in your life just as they are in heaven! May your children know and experience the Kingdom of God in your home. I pray that they will speak the Kingdom into their schools and pray heaven into the earth.

May all of God's purposes for your marriage be fulfilled on earth as it is in heaven.

1. What area of your family's life needs a heavenly invasion?

2. How can you participate in bringing the Kingdom into your home, school, workplace, community, and nation?

44

Surprises

Proverbs 3:5 (New International Version)

Trust in the LORD with all your heart and lean not on your own understanding

We trust in a Person, not in what we think we know! Our God has thoughts that are not our thoughts and ways that are not our ways. His thoughts and ways are not entirely revealed through principles. Intimacy with God is important so that we can hear, see, and sense His presence. I once asked a small group of church friends to comment on ways that God had surprised them in their lives. Not one person could think of one way that God had ever surprised them. That surprised me!

I want to commit to living a life that allows God to surprise me. When I look back on the year, I want to be able to see and know ways in which God revealed something that I didn't know, or took me to places I hadn't seen coming. I want to know that I am a different and emerging person than I was the year before because I have a God who surprises me. I want to trust Him with all my heart and never rely on what I think I know. Surprise me, God! Take me on an ever-unfolding adventure!

1. When we travel with God, we often leave the known for the unknown. There is often no map involved, but rather the need to listen for, watch, and follow God. In what ways has God surprised you on your journey?

2. What do you rely on? What do you put your trust in? How can you commit to the person of God rather than relying on what you think you know?

45

Whispers

Jeremiah 29:13 (New International Version)

You will seek me and find me when you seek me with all your heart.

When I want to speak to someone who is quite a distance across the room or down the street, I shout loudly! But when I want to speak intimately with someone, I whisper. When I'm in a knowing relationship with someone, I want to talk up close and speak about dear things. Whispering is the sound of intimacy. Sometimes I feel that the more God wants closeness with me, the more He whispers. I must come close to hear His intimate thoughts. There is no shouting because God wants no distance. We have a God who wants to be found and known, not from a distance, but close up. He wants me close so that He can speak in whispers and share His heart with me.

We seek you, God, with all our hearts. We lay at your feet. We seek to fully know and experience all of you—all of your facets and attributes. We want to know your provision, healing, safety, breakthrough, courage, peace, anointing, rest, knowledge, wisdom, blessing, and favor. We seek you. We pray that ALL of you will cover all of us!

1. Do you believe and understand the depth of God's desire to be near you? Pray that God will reveal to you how much He desires and loves you.

2. How can you seek God and come closer so you can hear His whispers? In what practical ways can you foster a more intimate, connected, and knowing relationship with the Father?

46

GIFT

JAMES 1:2-4 (THE MESSAGE)

Consider it a sheer gift, friends, when tests and challenges come at you from all sides. You know that under pressure, your faith-life is forced into the open and shows its true colors. So don't try to get out of anything prematurely. Let it do its work so you become mature and well-developed, not deficient in any way.

A lot of life is journey and process. During some seasons, things come at us from all sides. When your children are struggling, it can cut to the heart. There may be no easy solutions and no quick fixes. James assures us that tests and challenges come with gift, with joy. There is goodness that comes from wrestling with the things of life. A work is done in us to make sure that there is nothing undone, deficient, or lacking in our inner core and faith. The work makes certain that the things we need to be free from are brought to the surface and surrendered. The good work makes sure that the gold is tested and found pure, brilliant, and full of luster.

On the other side of struggle, we can see some of the good outcome, the value of the process. I encourage you to count it all joy, friends. I believe this season will leave you with stronger faith, more freedom, and new encounters with the Living God. Consider your challenges and obstacles as opportunities to embrace a Living God, to see more of His glory, and to come out in the end strengthened and overflowing with gift.

1. I do not believe that illness is ever sent by God to test us or teach us a lesson. However, our response to the struggles of this life involves wrestling, lessons, and gifts. What is your story? Have you seen a good work come out of struggle?

2. How can we show our children how to respond to challenges and obstacles? How can we invite them to meet a Living God in this and every situation?

47

Without Words

Romans 8:26-27 (Contemporary English Version)

In certain ways we are weak, but the Spirit is here to help us. For example, when we don't know what to pray for, the Spirit prays for us in ways that cannot be put into words. All of our thoughts are known to God. He can understand what is in the mind of the Spirit, as the Spirit prays for God's people.

Have you ever prayed relentlessly, only to find yourself without words anymore…emptied of thoughts, prayers, and direction? This scripture is so encouraging for those moments and seasons. The Spirit is interceding for us with prayers and intercessions that have no words; He joins us in our groaning and calling out. He knows the prayers that are needed, the strategy, and the focus for effective intercession.

How should I pray for this child? I have asked myself this question. What is God saying over my child? How did God want Mary to pray for Jesus as a child? Did He want her, for example, to pray for safety, health, or success? Or, were God's words over Jesus somehow different and more than that? I believe God is speaking a specific word over your child, but how can you join God in declaring His words over your young one? The spirit of God joins you in your intercessions, even picking up praying where you leave off, and directing your prayers in a way that is in agreement with what God is declaring and doing.

1. Think of a recent occasion when you prayed for someone and felt at a loss for words or direction. Meditate on this scripture, and trust the Spirit to pray into that situation for you.

2. Have you ever felt led by the Spirit to pray with a specific focus for someone else? Think about that situation and journal about how God entered into that circumstance.

48

A Name Spoken

1 Kings 13:1-3 (New International Version)

By the word of the LORD a man of God came from Judah to Bethel, as Jeroboam was standing by the altar to make an offering. By the word of the LORD he cried out against the altar: "Altar, altar! This is what the LORD says: 'A son named Josiah will be born to the house of David. On you he will sacrifice the priests of the high places who make offerings here, and human bones will be burned on you.'" That same day the man of God gave a sign: "This is the sign the LORD has declared: The altar will be split apart and the ashes on it will be poured out."

In this passage, an unnamed prophet comes to Bethel just as the king was about to offer pagan sacrifices at the altar. The prophet declares that a child will be born whose name will be Josiah. He will be born a descendant of King David, and he will restore right sacrifice and destroy the pagan rituals. Nearly three hundred years later, an eight-year-old boy named Josiah became king after the assassination of his father Amon. In the eighteenth year of his rule, Josiah ordered the renovation of the temple. During this time, the high priest Hilkiah discovered a copy of the ancient scriptures while he was clearing the treasure room within the temple structure. King Josiah ordered the scroll to be read aloud to the people. In the reading of the scripture, Josiah was convicted to restore the holiness of God's temple.

We don't know for sure what was contained in the scroll that was read aloud to the people, but consider the possibility that Josiah heard the prophetic decree made by the unnamed prophet at Bethel. Consider that he heard his name contained in the prophecy of the scriptures, and heard about his destiny in restoring right relationship between the people and God. Did he suddenly realize and understand that God had a plan for his life? Did he then know in the deepest recesses of his heart that God had spoken his name hundreds of years before he was born? Did he realize that the desire deep in his heart to restore the temple was a purpose breathed over him by the eternal God?

I believe that God speaks future and purpose over every single person. He knows, sees, and speaks into existence every person's identity in Christ. Might you be the answer to someone's prayer—someone's cry in the night? Might your child be the subject of declarations hundreds and hundreds of years old? Has God whispered the destiny and purpose of your family members to others separated by years and miles? When God whispered eternal secrets to His people, did He speak your name into the atmosphere and declare your identity over the hearts of His people?

1. Do you believe that God knows you and sees you? Do you believe that you have an identity in Christ that is meant to be impactful, vibrant, and world changing?

2. How can you help your child know and understand his/her identity and purpose in God's good plan? In what practical ways can you raise children to know that they are destined to impact their world for good?

49

Knowing

Daniel 11:32 (Amplified Bible)

The people who know their God shall prove themselves strong and shall stand firm and do exploits {for God}.

What does it mean to know God? Do you know the president? Do you know your pastor? Do you know your mother? Do you know your spouse, child, or yourself? There are different levels of knowing, aren't there? I believe that intimacy is a place of knowing and being known. What an amazing God we have: a God who wants to reveal Himself, who wants to be known, heard, and seen. There is no deceit in Him, no falsehood. He wants us to know Him, not just about Him. Through and through, and across the ages, He wants us to know Him deeply, intimately, and experientially.

Do you know God? Do you know God better than you know anyone else? Scripture says that *knowing God* will reveal itself as strength and the ability to stand firm. Those who know their God will do great things. They will endure, prosper, and stay true. The knowing is important. It cannot be bypassed. There is no substitution for knowing Him intimately, personally, and across time. Know your God.

1. Who do you know better than God, and why?

2. How can you know and be known by God in greater ways this season?

50

GOD, MY GLORY

PSALM 3:1-5 (AMPLIFIED BIBLE)

LORD, how they are increased who trouble me! Many are they who rise up against me. Many are saying of me, There is no help for him in God. Selah {pause, and calmly think of that}! But You, O Lord, are a shield for me, my glory, and the lifter of my head. With my voice I cry to the Lord, and He hears and answers me out of His holy hill. Selah {pause, and calmly think of that}! I lay down and slept; I wakened again, for the Lord sustains me.

So many times, I have felt surrounded by enemies—the things in life that seem to work against the welfare of my family. It is so easy to hear the voices saying, "God won't come through for you. Even God can't help. He is so far away from you..." That's why I love Psalm 3: It begins with these same thoughts and then responds, "But you, O Lord!" But you, O Lord! There is none like you. You protect me and encircle me. You are my glory, my shining treasure. You are the Lifter of my head! Oh, how I need someone to lift up my head! God is the One. He is our glory and the Lifter of our heads!

I cry out to Him, and He answers me. He is so ever present and responsive. He speaks to my heart in so many languages. Not only does He answer my questions, He *is* the Answer. He is the Answer to every question. As His goodness crowns me, I know the Answer. As He lifts up my head, I know the Answer. Then I am secure and at peace. Then I can rest and sleep, for God watches over me.

1. Let's pray together, reader. *God, I pray over this man, this woman, right now. I pray over his heart and her circumstance. I pray that each reader will know you as the lifter of his head, the Answer to her need! Be present to them, God, and encircle their little ones with glory, protecting them from darkness.*

2. What enemies are you facing? Invite God to be the lifter of your head this week. Journal about your experiences as God interacts with you.

51

REST

JOSHUA 21:43-44 (NEW INTERNATIONAL VERSION)

So the LORD gave Israel all the land he had sworn to give their ancestors, and they took possession of it and settled there. The LORD gave them rest on every side, just as he had sworn to their ancestors. Not one of their enemies withstood them; the LORD gave all their enemies into their hands.

I love these verses in the book of Joshua. The story is about the Israelites coming into the Promised Land. What a long journey for them. It was a physical journey as well as a journey of the mind, heart, and spirit. They encountered obstacles and challenges. They had failures and successes along the way. These verses describe the outcome.

Not only did the Lord give them the land He had promised, but he also gave them REST on every side. The Israelites had defeated all of their enemies, and they were surrounded by rest and peace. The striving and conflict had ceased. None of their enemies were left standing.

Whenever I read about "enemies" in the scripture, I like to think about what our enemies are. We don't encounter many Hittites or Amorites these days, but we do encounter enemies to be defeated such as fear, poverty, illness, depression, conflict, loneliness, and betrayal.

Let's pray together for "rest on every side": *We pray, God, that you will help us conquer all the enemies that come against our families and communities. We pray for rest on every side, as we take possession of the Promised Land and settle into it!*

1. What enemies do you and your family face?

2. What role does God have in conquering your enemies and giving you rest?

52

Legacy

Psalm 78:3-4 (Contemporary English Version)

These are things we learned from our ancestors, and we will tell them to the next generation. We won't keep secret the glorious deeds and the mighty miracles of the Lord.

What legacy will you leave your children? We have the opportunity to gift our children with a spiritual inheritance, a generational story, and the eternal heartbeat of God woven into their lives and the lives of His people. How has God impacted your family and the genealogy of your family tree? How is His painting reflected in your lives, His poetry spoken over the generations of your family? God's story is always meant to be an inheritance, to live through the lives of the next generation. It is gift, a treasure, and a golden revelation. God is always telling His story. How has He spoken into your family's life?

I invite you to think about the story of God in your life and begin telling your story. Tell of God's mighty deeds and power in the midst of unexpected trials and giant obstacles. May His wonders in your life always be on your lips. May the next generation know how God appeared in your life and changed things for good. His mighty deeds will live forever on the lips of His people.

1. Think about God's glorious deeds in the lives of your ancestors and the generations that have come before you. Think about God's presence in your own life—His revelations and interventions.

2. How can you tell the next generation about your journey with God? Think of a practical way to do this and pursue it this month.

53

Don't Stumble

Luke 7:20-23 (New International Version)

When the men came to Jesus, they said, "John the Baptist sent us to you to ask, 'Are you the one who is to come, or should we expect someone else?'" At that very time Jesus cured many who had diseases, sicknesses and evil spirits, and gave sight to many who were blind. So he replied to the messengers, "Go back and report to John what you have seen and heard: The blind receive sight, the lame walk, those who have leprosy are cleansed, the deaf hear, the dead are raised, and the good news is proclaimed to the poor. Blessed is anyone who does not stumble on account of me."

I can only imagine the mental and emotional process of John the Baptist as he lay in prison while Jesus began His ministry...healing and setting other people free. John sent his friends to clarify whether Jesus was even the Messiah, something John himself had declared earlier at Jesus's baptism. John must have begun to doubt everything he thought he had known. I believe he wrestled with the "why" of his current situation, as he lay in prison while Jesus set other people free.

Jesus's response to this emotional wrestling is poignant. He tells the disciples to tell John all about the miracles occurring in fulfillment of the scriptures referring to the Messiah's mission (see Isaiah 61). Then He gets to the heart of the matter. Jesus says, "Blessed is anyone who does not stumble on account of me." He sees John's heart and knows his wrestling. He encourages him not to stumble. Don't stumble John. Don't stumble. Don't let your wrestling become an issue that keeps you from the truth.

When you or your children are struggling, it is so easy to stumble, to take offense at the injustice of the way life is playing out. Some things in this life are not fixed or restored, not as they will be some day. There is tension in the "in between place" of hungering and thirsting for rightness, peace, joy, healing…all the qualities of the Kingdom, and yet not living in that place completely. Can we live in the tension without stumbling? Can we give God our love and trust, even when things are unfixed and incomplete?

1. In what ways are you tempted to stumble when you see things in the lives of your children and family that are unjust and unfixed?

2. How do you balance your hunger and thirst for rightness with the tension of the here and now?

3. Is there any area of your life that has led you into offense or stumbling? Do you feel a lack of forgiveness toward God? How can you move from offense into trust and forgiveness?

54

Stand

Ephesians 6:10-13 (New International Version)

Finally, be strong in the Lord and in his mighty power. Put on the full armor of God, so that you can take your stand against the devil's schemes. For our struggle is not against flesh and blood, but against the rulers, against the authorities, against the powers of this dark world and against the spiritual forces of evil in the heavenly realms. Therefore put on the full armor of God, so that when the day of evil comes, you may be able to stand your ground, and after you have done everything, to stand.

I believe that everyone on some level understands that there is a power to darkness. This passage of scripture talks about our struggles in this life. We come against spiritual forces that have authority, strategy, and power in the dark realms of this age. It is the ancient story of good versus evil.

It is difficult, as parents, to watch our children struggle, whether that involves health, comfort, relationships, learning, or peace of mind. We struggle and wrestle too, praying and problem-solving. It is important to know that when we struggle, it is not ultimately against other people, organizations, laws, or fate. In the end, we wrestle with spiritual forces of darkness. Ephesians 6 encourages us to be empowered and filled with strength, not through our own energy, but by drawing power from the connection we have with the God of the Universe. When we have done all that we know to do, we stand our ground. Stand. Don't back down from darkness, don't run away, don't hide...just stand with God. In the end, evil does not win.

1. Have there been seasons in your journey when you wrestled with darkness?

2. Did you recognize the struggle between good and evil? How did you take a stand for good?

3. How do you teach your children to stand for good in the midst of darkness and struggle?

55

Defense of the City

Isaiah 37:33-35 (New International Version)

"Therefore this is what the LORD says concerning the king of Assyria: "He will not enter this city or shoot an arrow here. He will not come before it with shield or build a siege ramp against it. By the way that he came he will return; he will not enter this city," declares the LORD. "I will defend this city and save it, for my sake and for the sake of David my servant!"

When I was pregnant with my son, I was exhausted and nauseous for the first four to five months. Sometimes, all I could do was lie in bed on the weekends, trying to recoup for the next week. There were several things going on in my extended family during that time that needed prayer. I remember reading this passage in Isaiah and praying it over my family members across the country as I lay in bed. "This is what God says! The enemy can't have this city. No arrow will leave the quiver, no shield come against it. There will be no siege. The enemy will leave the same way it came, without accomplishing anything. God will defend the city and save it because of who He is and all of His promises!"

Picture this: The Assyrian army camped outside of Jerusalem's walls. The Assyrians were a formidable and beastly army. They were shouting taunts and threats outside the wall, saying that no one could save the Jewish people, not King Hezekiah or the Lord their God. For it was said that the Assyrians had never been defeated in battle. But the Jewish people did trust in God when He said that the enemy wouldn't take the city. That night, an angel of the Lord went through the enemy camp and killed 185,000 enemy soldiers. The people listened to God and trusted His word. They did not have to fight the battle themselves. God defended them. The King of Assyria turned and went home.

1. Trust in God and His promises. I invite you to pray this prayer over your household. The enemy can't have your family. God will defend and save you.

2. I believe there is spiritual power in speaking God's own words over your family. What is He saying about your situation? Speak His promises in faith and power.

56

JOY

NEHEMIAH 8:9-12 (AMPLIFIED BIBLE)

And Nehemiah, who was the governor, and Ezra the priest and scribe, and the Levites who taught the people said to all of them, This day is holy to the Lord your God; mourn not nor weep. For all the people wept when they heard the words of the Law. Then {Ezra} told them, Go your way, eat the fat, drink the sweet drink, and send portions to him for whom nothing is prepared; for this day is holy to our Lord. And be not grieved and depressed, for the joy of the Lord is your strength and stronghold. So the Levites quieted all the people, saying, Be still, for the day is holy. And do not be grieved and sad. And all the people went their way to eat, drink, send portions, and make great rejoicing, for they had understood the words that were declared to them.

Nehemiah was governor of Judah between approximately 445-433 BCE. He initiated the movement to rebuild the walls around Jerusalem, an effort that had not been undertaken even after the exiles had been back in Jerusalem from Babylon for about eighty years. Ezra was a priest and scribe. Together, Nehemiah and Ezra were urging the exiles to return to their national and spiritual heritage in the land. This scripture includes Ezra's reading of the law before the people. Upon hearing the word of God, the people began to weep because they realized their lives didn't reflect God's will for them.

Interestingly, the response of Nehemiah and Ezra was to encourage them to feast and celebrate, for "the joy of the Lord is your strength!" The Levites (priests) also said, "Don't weep! For this is a sacred day." Sometimes we think of holy and sacred things being serious and perhaps mournful. The idea of laughing in church or celebrating and feasting upon hearing the word of God may seem somewhat disrespectful. Somehow, a serious-minded approach can seem more holy. But here we see something different. Read the last verse above: "And all the people went their way to eat, drink, send portions, and make great rejoicing, for they had understood the words that were declared to them." When we hear God's words and understand them, we know that at the foundation of all that God does, there is joy and celebration! We celebrate His goodness. We rejoice in His loving kindness. We abound in hope by the power of the Spirit. We know that the joy of the Lord is our strength!

1. What is the joy of the Lord? How does it contrast with our sometimes "serious-minded" Sundays? Who is the God of the Bible that laughs, sings, and dances?

2. How can you celebrate the joy of God today? Have you laughed, danced, or feasted today? I encourage you to celebrate God's goodness with your children. May the joy of the Lord strengthen you today.

57

Remove Obstacles

Isaiah 57:14 (The Message)

Someone says, "Build, build! Make a road! Clear the way, remove the rocks from the road my people will travel."

You and your children are on a journey. You are traveling a great distance across formidable territory. You don't have a map, and at times, there is no defined path. Perhaps no one has walked this particular way before. Your shoes are wearing thin, and your feet hurt. You feel weary, tired, and hungry. Yet, someone says, "Build, build, build. Make a road and clear the way! Remove all the obstacles from the path of travel. Clear the way!"

Let's pray that all obstacles to health, joy, kingdom living, and relationships will be removed from your path, and that you will experience breakthrough. Let's pray for building and raising up. Let's pray for an open road and a clearing of the way. May all obstacles be removed. I pray over your journey, dear ones!

1. What path are you traveling? How has the journey been for you and your children?

2. What obstacles need to be removed from your path? Let's pray together today, right now, for a clearing of the way!

58

Preparation

1 Samuel 17:32-35, 37 (Contemporary English Version)

"Your Majesty," he (David) said, "this Philistine shouldn't turn us into cowards. I'll go out and fight him myself!" "You don't have a chance against him," Saul replied. "You're only a boy, and he's been a soldier all his life." But David told him: Your Majesty, I take care of my father's sheep. And when one of them is dragged off by a lion or a bear, I go after it and beat the wild animal until it lets the sheep go. If the wild animal turns and attacks me, I grab it by the throat and kill it...The LORD has rescued me from the claws of lions and bears, and he will keep me safe from the hands of this Philistine."

David and Goliath—what a wonderful story about an "unqualified" youth fighting the giant that no one could face. I encourage you to read the whole story again, but let's meditate together on these verses for a moment. What is the giant in your circumstance that taunts your community, your church, or your kids? Is it the giant of cancer, pain, hopelessness, abuse, poverty, or autism? Has anyone been able to defeat this giant and bring it down? Do you feel qualified to do just that?

Many times, when something enters our lives that is unexpected and overwhelming, we feel "unprepared." We may say, "This is not how I thought my life would be. Nothing has prepared me for this." In 1 Samuel, King Saul is letting David know that he is not qualified to fight Goliath, as he has had no preparation, no training. David responds that his life as a shepherd has trained him to be a warrior. In fact, his whole life has prepared him for this moment.

When we are taunted by a giant in our own circumstances, we may feel unprepared and at a loss. We may see children struggling and not know what to do to help. Often times, however, if we stop and look back through our lives, we come to see that the whole journey has prepared us for the current moment in many critical ways. We may not have all the answers, but in pivotal ways, we are armed, prepared, and ready to defeat the enemy.

1. Identify a Goliath in your life right now.

2. Look back on your life's journey. How has God prepared you to defeat this giant?

59

NO WEAPON

ISAIAH 54:17 (AMPLIFIED BIBLE)

But no weapon that is formed against you shall prosper, and every tongue that shall rise against you in judgment you shall show to be in the wrong. This {peace, righteousness, security, triumph over opposition} is the heritage of the servants of the Lord {those in whom the ideal Servant of the Lord is reproduced}; this is the righteousness or the vindication which they obtain from Me {this is that which I impart to them as their justification}, says the Lord.

There is no weapon formed against the servants of God that can prosper. No weapon formed against you or your household shall thrive or progress. Everything that rises against you from darkness will be shown to be in the wrong. Why? Because you will rise up in the glory and rightness of God. You will rise into your God-given future and show that your heritage from the Lord is peace, safety, righteousness, and triumph over opposition. This is your heritage from God. Weapons will fall apart around you as God's glory covers you.

This passage reminds me of the saying "Living well is the best revenge." When darkness rises against us in judgment and weapons are formed against us, the peace and victory of God, which is our inheritance, will shine forth. Our living in God's glory is our vindication and heritage from the Lord. In this context, everything formed against us falls apart, and false judgments are shown to be wrong.

1. What oppositions or weapons have you seen come against you or your family? What darkness have you felt come against you?

2. I encourage you to pray this scripture over your household today. No weapon formed against your household shall thrive or prosper. All will fall apart in the presence of the glorious God who gives you peace and victory in the midst of darkness.

60

True Self

John 4:23-24 (The Message)

"It's who you are and the way you live that count before God. Your worship must engage your spirit in the pursuit of truth. That's the kind of people the Father is out looking for: those who are simply and honestly themselves before him in their worship. God is sheer being itself—Spirit. Those who worship him must do it out of their very being, their spirits, their true selves, in adoration."

God loves your heart and your genuine humanity. He loves to see the real you and watch as you lay your true self at his feet. He wants intimacy with you, in truth…the intimacy of you knowing Him and of you being known by Him. He wants to be near you today. He doesn't want to wait for some future time when you feel more "prepared" or more "ready" to engage with Him. He wants your heart now…the real heart, filled with such a mixture of emotions and questions. It is intimacy when you present yourself before Him and lie at His feet. Worship Him in that place. Let Him know you. Let Him invite you into Himself. He longs to be close to you.

1. Allow God to sing over you today. Come before Him in truth and lie at His feet.

2. As you worship God in truth, what does He say to you? Keep a journal of your insights during this time. Ask God to reveal His truth to you. Ask Him who He is. Ask Him who you are.

61

SPEAK

ESTHER 4:14 (AMPLIFIED BIBLE)

For if you keep silent at this time, relief and deliverance shall arise for the Jews from elsewhere, but you and your father's house will perish. And who knows but that you have come to the kingdom for such a time as this and for this very occasion?

It takes wisdom to know when to keep silent and when to rise up and speak. In the book of Esther, a young girl is unexpectedly taken into the King's harem, finds favor, and becomes Queen. She is a Jew, but she has kept her heritage a secret. There arises in the kingdom a threat to the lives of the Jewish people. This is a crossroads for Esther. Does she reveal herself by standing up to speak for the Jews, or does she remain hidden. In this verse, her relative, Mordecai, encourages her to speak. He says, "…who knows but that you have come to the kingdom for such a time as this and for this very occasion?"

When we find ourselves in the middle of a battle, we have a choice. We can shut down and disappear in silence, or we can stand up and speak. We can speak out against the darkness. We can speak life over people around us. We can share testimony about our struggles, challenges, and God's work in the midst of the crisis. The choice is between isolation and community, between silence and speaking, between privacy and connection. Mordecai emphasizes that deliverance for the Jewish community would come regardless of Esther's decision; however, her ability to engage in the kingdom and to come into her identity and destiny would be determined by her own choices about becoming involved and speaking out.

1. As a parent of a child with special needs, you have found yourself in a position that you did not envision. Perhaps you have come to the Kingdom for such a time as this. How can you advocate for children and parents in this situation? What practical steps can you take to speak out, get involved, and contend for breakthrough?

2. How can your children step into their Kingdom destinies within their current situations? How can you encourage them in their journey to get involved and be a blessing to others?

62

Most Real

Daniel 10:12-13 (The Message)

"'Relax, Daniel," he continued, "don't be afraid. From the moment you decided to humble yourself to receive understanding, your prayer was heard, and I set out to come to you. But I was waylaid by the angel-prince of the kingdom of Persia and was delayed for a good three weeks. But then Michael, one of the chief angel-princes, intervened to help me. I left him there with the prince of the kingdom of Persia."

In this text, Daniel had been fasting and praying for the discernment of the visions he had received in the spiritual realm. The "man" speaking to him is an angel—one that many believe to be Gabriel. The moment Daniel prayed, God listened to him, but the answer to his prayer was delayed because of an angelic battle. Michael, the archangel, came to assist in the battle, and the angel eventually made it to Daniel's side to bring understanding from God.

This is a glimpse into the unseen realm described by scripture. It highlights that prayer is heard by God, and that intercessions release responses in your life. As described here, sometimes the responses are delayed because of things you can't see. This scripture also highlights some of the conflict in the unseen realm between spiritual forces. Be encouraged, reader, that your prayers are powerful. When you speak prayer into the atmosphere, spiritual reality is impacted in ways you may not see. There may seem to be delay or disregard in the heavens. However, what you can't see is more real than what you can see.

1. Do you feel that your prayers are heard and have an impact on the spiritual environment?

2. Let's pray together. *Lord, I pray for the reader right now. I pray over his mind, spirit, and heart. I pray that she will know, in a real way, the breakthrough power of her intercessions today! I pray, God, that you will reveal the unseen and allow your children, young and old, to know what is most real today.*

63

STAY

EXODUS 33:7, 11 (THE MESSAGE)

Moses used to take the Tent and set it up outside the camp, some distance away. He called it the Tent of Meeting. Anyone who sought God would go to the Tent of Meeting outside the camp...And God spoke with Moses face-to-face, as neighbors speak to one another. When he would return to the camp, his attendant, the young man Joshua, stayed—he didn't leave the Tent.

To me, every sentence in this passage unfolds as more spectacular than the one before it. Moses set up a tent where people could meet with the manifest Presence of God. Anyone who sought God could go to the tent and meet with Him, and they could abide there with the manifest Presence of God. They could inquire of God for answers, ask for revelations, and pray for provision. Or, they could just abide there, without talking, just being with their Creator. The tent was a place to be, meet, and abide with God.

The scripture says that there in the tent, Moses would actually go and meet face to face with God, as friends and neighbors speak to each other. Just as you might go get coffee with a friend, Moses went and visited with God Almighty. Amazing, and when Moses was finished and went home, what did Joshua do? He stayed. He didn't leave the tent.

We are invited to meet with God face to face, to abide with Him, to be in intimate relationship with the Lord. May we have the heart of Moses, running after God until we see Him face to face. May we have the passion and love of Joshua, staying, when even Moses has gone home. May we have the heart to stay in the Presence of the loving God, never leaving.

1. This scripture says that whoever wanted to seek the Lord was invited to the tent. In what ways do you want to seek Him? Do you have needs on your heart—prayers for your child and your household? Present them before Him today.

2. I pray for your heart. May you and your children have such love and passion for God, that you find yourself staying at the tent when everyone else has gone home, never leaving, abiding forever in His Presence.

64

WALK

ISAIAH 40:31 (AMPLIFIED BIBLE)

But those who wait for the Lord {who expect, look for, and hope in Him} shall change and renew their strength and power; they shall lift their wings and mount up {close to God} as eagles {mount up to the sun}; they shall run and not be weary, they shall walk and not faint or become tired.

Life can feel strenuous. As I pray and work for breakthrough for my child, I can easily feel the rigor of the pace and the need for endurance. I love this passage from Isaiah. Read it with me. Are you waiting for the Lord, expecting, looking for, and hoping? Do you wait expectantly for Him to come with breakthrough, provision, and healing?

Hebrew poetry is rhythmic in many ways. When a sequence is presented like this in scripture, the simplest piece is usually presented first, and then the subsequent pieces become increasingly amazing and glorious. Here we see that those who wait on the Lord will fly up to God, run and not be weary, and walk and not tire. The sequence is interesting because we may have thought walking would be first because it is the simplest, and then perhaps progressing to flying—the most glorious. But the verse identifies walking as the most amazing piece, the glorious culmination of the sequence. This makes sense, doesn't it? It is often walking, the day-to-day routine, that is the most strenuous and difficult. How amazing that when we expect and hope in God, we shall walk and not faint! How glorious and wonderful! God is with us when we need endurance for the daily walk.

1. In what areas of your life are you waiting on God? Are you able to wait with expectation and hope?

2. How have you seen God give you endurance for your daily walk?

65

SABBATH

PSALM 127:1-2 (CONTEMPORARY ENGLISH VERSION)

Without the help of the LORD it is useless to build a home or to guard a city. It is useless to get up early and stay up late in order to earn a living. God takes care of his own, even while they sleep.

Households are generally busy places. There are typically several people, all with multiple needs and schedules throughout the week. For parents of children with extraordinary needs, the demands may even be more intense, the schedules much more filled, and the juggling more difficult. You may find yourself burning the candle at both ends and feeling that several things are getting lost in the shuffle. You may feel like you are just trying to hold things together. You may be in survival-mode much of the time.

Let's pray through the beginning of Psalm 127. Here, it reminds us that trying to build or guard without the help of God is "useless." This is an example in scripture of the concept that God wants to partner with humans to produce good things on earth—to usher in the Kingdom. These verses also emphasize the importance of rest. God knows you need rest for health and balance. God recognized the need for rest by setting the example (i.e., resting on the seventh day of creation) and creating the Sabbath. Not only is rest imperative, but it also is an expression of faith. There is a high level of trust demonstrated when we can rest, even when things aren't done or fixed yet! When we rest, we must trust that God will help meet our needs—that He will help us build, guard, survive, and thrive.

1. How easy is it for you to rest when things are not complete? How often are you able to set time aside to rest, worship, and Sabbath?

2. How much does your faith and trust in God impact how often you rest?

66

Prayers Left Behind

Luke 1:13 (New International Version)

But the angel said to him: "Do not be afraid, Zechariah; your prayer has been heard. Your wife Elizabeth will bear you a son, and you are to call him John."

The book of Luke begins with the Christmas story—first with the birth of John the Baptist, and then with the birth of Messiah, Jesus. Here we see John's father, Zechariah, childless and of an old age, chosen by lot to burn incense in the inner temple. It is here that he encounters an angel of the Lord. The angel tells Zechariah that his prayer has been heard, his prayer for a child, the prayer he prayed long ago as a young man. The prayer he no longer prays. In fact, Zechariah challenges the angel, asking how this could possibly be true. He is too old, the prayer itself is from long ago, and the time for the prayer to be fulfilled has seemingly passed. But, the angel says that the prayer Zechariah no longer prays has been heard and answered. In fact, Zechariah's name itself means, "God has remembered."

What prayers have you lost hope for? What prayers do you no longer pray? I pray that you will know that your prayers are heard and remembered by God today. I pray that the resurrection God will resurrect hope in you for intervention now, and that you will see miracles beyond your wildest expectation. *God, we pray for fruitfulness where there once was barrenness. Thank you for being a God who remembers the prayers that we have left behind.*

1. Is there a prayer that you no longer pray because you have given up hope? Can you relate to how skeptical Zechariah felt in that moment, in his "old age?"

2. Is there any prayer you feel that God wants to resurrect and bring to life again? I pray that He will guide your prayers and fill you with hope for new breakthrough.

67

Battle Strategy

2 Chronicles 20:21-22 (New International Version)

Jehoshaphat appointed men to sing to the LORD and to praise him for the splendor of his holiness as they went out at the head of the army, saying: "Give thanks to the LORD, for his love endures forever." As they began to sing and praise, the LORD set ambushes against the men of Ammon and Moab and Mount Seir who were invading Judah, and they were defeated.

I encourage you to read the story of Jehoshaphat, King of Judah, in 2 Chronicles chapter 20. This is just one story in the scriptures involving an unusual battle strategy. As parents of children with persistent challenges, we often find ourselves in need of a battle strategy to problem solve a challenge or overcome an obstacle. It is interesting to read about God's history with battle strategies.

Early in the chapter, Jehoshaphat is told that a "vast army" is coming against him (have you ever felt that way?). He proclaimed a fast, and the people of Judah came together to seek the Lord. This was the word of the Lord to them: "Do not be afraid or discouraged because of this vast army. For the battle is not yours, but God's." The people of Judah were instructed to go and face the enemy; God would be with them.

King Jehoshaphat sent the praise and worship team out ahead of the army to sing the praises of God! When they reached the battlefield, the enemy factions turned on each other and destroyed themselves. All that was left was for the people of Judah to take the plunder.

Are you in need of a battle strategy? Seek the Lord and listen to Him! He has some interesting strategies for approaching the battlefield. Perhaps you will be like Jehoshaphat, who came to meet the enemy with praise and worship in the lead, only to see the enemy destroy itself.

1. In what area of life are you seeking a battle strategy? What is the enemy that is coming against you or your family (e.g., illness, fear, financial struggle)?

2. Have you tried to face the enemy with praise and thanksgiving in your heart?

3. God may give other strategies. Can you remember a time that God gave you breakthrough in a situation through another strategy?

68

Never Denying

Psalm 84:11 (Contemporary English Version)

Our LORD and our God, you are like the sun and also like a shield. You treat us with kindness and with honor, never denying any good thing to those who live right.

The Lord your God is like the sun to you and your children. He covers you with warmth and light. He is your source of life, allowing you to grow and flourish. The Lord your God is like a shield to you and your household. He surrounds you with protection and defense. He does not leave you without covering. He shows you kindness. How kind is your God! He protects your heart and fills you up. He shows you honor, never shaming or crushing you. He lifts up your head and crowns you with His glory.

The Lord your God never denies you any good thing when you live uprightly in relationship with Him. His plans for you are good and abundant and meet your every need. He is the solution to every problem you face. He does not withhold any good thing from you.

Meditate on verse 11 today. I pray that you and your family will know these qualities of your God intimately and deeply. I pray it will change your life and your future. May you be released from everything that holds you bound; may you and your children know every freedom and abundance in God.

1. When life brings challenges and seasons of struggle, are you tempted to think that God is withholding good things from you and your family? What do you believe about God's character? Is He a withholding God? Ask God to reveal His character to you.

2. I pray that you and your household will know the light, the warmth, the kindness, the honor, and the protection of your God today! Recite this verse today and see what God does—what He reveals to your spirit.

69

SABBATH HEALING

LUKE 13:10-14 (CONTEMPORARY ENGLISH VERSION)

One Sabbath, Jesus was teaching in a Jewish meeting place, and a woman was there who had been crippled by an evil spirit for eighteen years. She was completely bent over and could not straighten up. When Jesus saw the woman, he called her over and said, "You are now well." He placed his hands on her, and right away she stood up straight and praised God. The man in charge of the meeting place was angry because Jesus had healed someone on the Sabbath. So he said to the people, "Each week has six days when we can work. Come and be healed on one of those days, but not on the Sabbath."

There are seven Sabbath miracles recorded in scripture, and they each have to do with healing and deliverance. I was meditating on this the other day and was so encouraged. I am a worker in my personality. In fact, my name means "industrious." I am efficient and capable when faced with problems and projects. There are times when that sweat is productive and important. However, I can struggle to find balance. I may find it difficult to rest and trust in the God of the universe. I could easily be one of those in this scripture story who argues that healing *should* somehow go along with work. How can one find healing and breakthrough when resting?!

I rejoice in you Jesus! You defy my reasoning and break into my work. You approach me through rest and trust. You *can* bring healing and deliverance during seasons when I set down my striving and lay at your feet. Let me just gaze on you, Jesus, and soak you in. I need to rest in your Presence and trust in Who you are. Total rest and trust in God. No striving or sweat. True gift, true grace! Jesus, you simply come on the scene and set people free, healing on the Sabbath! God amazes me.

1. Do you find it easier to work for breakthrough or to rest in God's presence? How do you find balance?

2. Have you ever met the God of Sabbath healing? Were you able to receive this gift from Him?

70

Great Work

Nehemiah 6: 1-3 (The Message)

When Sanballat, Tobiah, Geshem the Arab, and the rest of our enemies heard that I had rebuilt the wall and that there were no more breaks in it—even though I hadn't yet installed the gates— Sanballat and Geshem sent this message: "Come and meet with us at Kephirim in the valley of Ono." I knew they were scheming to hurt me so I sent messengers back with this: "I'm doing a great work; I can't come down. Why should the work come to a standstill just so I can come down to see you?"

In this story, Nehemiah was helping the Jewish people rebuild the city walls of Jerusalem. In that era, city walls were important to fortify and secure the city, keeping the people and the city resources safe from enemies. He faced opposition during the rebuilding process. His enemies tried to lure him away from the work. They wanted him to come down to the valley to meet, a trick to capture and hurt him. He replied, "I'm doing a great work; I can't come down. Why should the work come to a standstill just so I can come down to see you?"

Don't let enemies distract you from your great work. God has called us to join Him in His mission to proclaim good news to the despairing, comfort the brokenhearted, free the captives, and comfort those who mourn

(Isaiah 61). You may have heard God call you into additional specific areas of mission. Whatever your specific identity and destiny in Christ, you have been called to do a great work! Don't allow opposition to the rebuilding cause you to become distracted or discouraged. Don't go down to the valley. After all, why should the good work you have put your hand to come to a standstill?

1. Have you ever experienced opposition to a rebuilding work God has called you to do?

2. What approach helped you stay focused on the good work rather than going down to the valley and leaving the work undone?

71

Gentle Leading

Isaiah 40:11 (New International Version)

He tends his flock like a shepherd: He gathers the lambs in his arms and carries them close to his heart; he gently leads those that have young.

We are parents. We are trying to lead our young. We may approach this with ease or encounter hardship. Our children may excel or struggle in seasons. How is your parent-heart today? This scripture verse describes God as a Shepherd tending His flock. How does He tend to His people? He carries us close to His heart. He gently leads us with our young.

As we parent, we need leading and wisdom. We have a God who sees our young and us. He knows we need gentle leading. His heart is for us, and He carries us close. I pray that you will know your Shepherd today. That you will hear His heart as He carries you, feel His heart beating for you and for your children. May your eyes be open to His hand in your life and see the compassion and love He has for you and your children.

1. In what ways have you seen God's heart for you? Have you felt His gentle leading as you care for your children?

2. Spend quiet time with God today, asking Him to draw you to His heart in an experiential way. I pray that you will feel His real presence in a transforming way today.

72

Love

1 Corinthians 13:4-8 (New International Version)

Love is patient, love is kind. It does not envy, it does not boast, it is not proud. It does not dishonor others, it is not self-seeking, it is not easily angered, it keeps no record of wrongs. Love does not delight in evil but rejoices with the truth. It always protects, always trusts, always hopes, always perseveres. Love never fails.

It is important for me to meditate on who God is. If I let my circumstances or feelings dictate what I believe, I may meditate on what I lack, evil, or "what ifs." Let me meditate instead on that which is true and unfailing, the very character of the unchanging God. This passage from 1 Corinthians is often read at weddings and outlines the characteristics of love. We know that perfect love is found in God.

God is patient in all circumstances and with all people. He does not envy or boast; He is not prideful. He never dishonors you and is not self-seeking. He is slow to anger. He keeps no record of the wrongs you do. God does not delight in evil; He rejoices in the truth! God always protects. God always trusts. God always hopes. God always perseveres. God never fails you!

1. What part of God's character strikes you the most in this passage?

2. Do you have a harder time believing God's character toward you or toward other people? Can you claim these promises for you, for your children, and for your household?

73

Meaningful Stones

Joshua 4:21-24 (New International Version)

He said to the Israelites, "In the future when your descendants ask their parents, 'What do these stones mean?' tell them, 'Israel crossed the Jordan on dry ground.' For the LORD your God dried up the Jordan before you until you had crossed over. The LORD your God did to the Jordan what he had done to the Red Sea when he dried it up before us until we had crossed over. He did this so that all the peoples of the earth might know that the hand of the LORD is powerful and so that you might always fear the LORD your God."

Do you have stories about God in your life? Ways that He has impressed something on your heart, answered prayer, or intervened in some impossible situation? In this scripture, Joshua is telling the people how important it is to record their experiences with God. "In the future your children will ask..."

We teach our children many things and in many ways. As parents of children who have specific needs, you may find that much of your life revolves around ways to help teach your children important things. I hope you know that there is nothing more important than sharing your experiences with

God with your kids. They will need to know what God has done in the past, to understand who He is and how He impacts life.

I used to have some stories in my head that I might tell or share if the occasion arose. Now I know better. I keep a journal to record every time I feel impacted by God. One reason I started the journal is to be able to share these experiences with my family. But I realized that as I have gone about this journey, the experiences of God are as much for my own sustenance and encouragement as they are for those around me. These stories testify to the truth! They resonate with the truth and life of Jesus Christ in everyday life. They testify to His character and His ways.

As I started writing, I also began to see that the process of recording my experiences trained me to notice more and more moments of God's presence. I became more sensitive to His promptings, interventions, and directions. The more I wrote them down, the more they sprang to life in my circumstances and world.

1. What are your experiences with God? Have you told them to others? Do you use them to sustain yourself?

2. Have you recorded these encounters? I invite you to keep a journal of impressions, interventions, and moments with God. I believe it will change your life and the lives of those around you.

74

HEALING SHADOW

ACTS 5:15 (CONTEMPORARY ENGLISH VERSION)

Then sick people were brought out to the road and placed on cots and mats. It was hoped that Peter would walk by, and his shadow would fall on them and heal them.

In the Old Testament, people lived with the understanding that things around them could make them "unclean." People who were ill, disabled, or had died, would contaminate the holiness of those who came in contact with them. In dramatic contrast, Jesus came onto the scene and introduced a New Covenant. He was seen touching the lepers, the sick, and the dead. His actions testified that the environment couldn't make us "unclean." We have the Spirit of God living in us. The environment can't change us, but we can change the environment.

Peter impacted the environment for Christ by merely walking among the people and allowing his shadow to cover them. His intimacy with God was so profound, and the Presence of God so powerful in his person, that the anointing was "infectious" to others. Peter's presence brought Christ's Presence to the environment.

Be intimate with God today. Know that God fills you with His glory so that you can walk among His people and impact the environment for good. You are called to bring a Christ-like and joyous atmosphere wherever you go!

1. In what way can your presence bring Christ to an environment that is hungry for Him?

2. When you sense fear, despair, and anger around you, how can you release God's Spirit to permeate and change the atmosphere?

75

Relationship

Luke 15:11-13 (Amplified Bible)

And He said, There was a certain man who had two sons; And the younger of them said to his father, Father, give me the part of the property that falls {to me}. And he divided the estate between them. And not many days after that, the younger son gathered up all that he had and journeyed into a distant country, and there he wasted his fortune in reckless and loose {from restraint} living.

The father had two sons. The older son had a relationship with the rules. The younger son had a relationship with his father's property. Who had a relationship with the father? Who chose father over property, rules, inheritance, and justification? However, the father wanted relationship with his sons. When his youngest son was still a long way off, the father ran out to him and threw his arms around him, restoring the son's place in the family, calling for a party! When the older son was angry because the rules for right behavior had been broken, the father came outside to him and asked him to come into the household and join in the family celebration.

No matter what we are attached to, God is always inviting us back into the house, into the family, into relationship with Him. He longs for relationship with you, even when the rules have been broken and the property is gone. He wants you. He wants your children. He wants to be close to you, to speak intimately with you of eternal things. What do you want? Can we say we want the Father completely, without offense or reservation, and that nothing else comes first?

1. Are relationships at the top of your priority list? How is your relationship with God? Does it need tending, commitment, or time? How can you pay attention to that relationship today?

2. In what ways can we show our children that relationships and people come first? How can we consistently invite them into the household, no matter what? How can we help them demonstrate that love and relationship to others?

76

Blessing Prayer

Numbers 6:24-27 (Amplified Bible)

The Lord bless you and watch, guard, and keep you; The Lord make His face to shine upon and enlighten you and be gracious (kind, merciful, and giving favor) to you; The Lord lift up His {approving} countenance upon you and give you peace (tranquility of heart and life continually). And they shall put My name upon the Israelites, and I will bless them.

You may be familiar with this blessing prayer from the book of Numbers. Some households use this scripture as a family prayer to bless each child and parent. I want you to know today, reader, that there are people praying for you that you don't even know about. I am praying for you. I pray this over you as a blessing.

Reader, I pray that the Lord will forever and in every way be a blessing in your life. I see Him watching you, guarding, and keeping you. I pray that you will experience His face shining upon you and your life. I pray that He will enlighten your spirit and fill you with His grace. The Lord is a gracious God; He is so kind and merciful to you. I pray that you will see His favor on your life, on the lives of your children, and each of those you love. May you know the deep transcendent peace of God—the tranquility of heart that brings continual life. The Lord covers you with His very Name, His complete person and character, and all of His blessings.

1. Who do you pray for continually? Do you have a blessing prayer for them?

2. Who prays over your life? Do you know that there are people praying for you who do so in the silent places? You are the beloved of God! May you and your children be fully blessed.

77

Glory Strength

Colossians 1:11-12 (The Message)

We pray that you'll have the strength to stick it out over the long haul—not the grim strength of gritting your teeth but the glory-strength God gives. It is strength that endures the unendurable and spills over into joy, thanking the Father who makes us strong enough to take part in everything bright and beautiful that he has for us.

There are seasons marked by the need for endurance. Sometimes you may feel like you are running a sprint, and other times you know you are running a marathon. In this passage, Paul is praying for believers that need strength for the long haul, the marathon. I love the word pictures in this translation. The contrast is made between grim-strength and glory-strength! I know you have felt grim-strength before—the kind that wears you down and tightens you up, weakening you over time. But God provides glory-strength—the kind of strength that endures and then spills over into joy! That is supernatural strength and endurance for sure, and it is available to you through God.

Let's pray together over your life right now. *Father God, we pray that you will breathe over the lives of your children, young and old. We pray that as they come into a close knowing relationship with you, they will know endurance beyond the natural. I pray that even now, even today, things will become "too easy!" I pray that strength will actually spill over and flow into joy for each reader and the ones they love.*

1. What would make your situation "too easy" today? Pray for a breakthrough in that area.

2. Take time to rest in God today. I challenge you to spend thirty minutes soaking in God's Spirit today. Lie down, turn your mind off, and invite God to surround you, renew you, and strengthen you.

78

Name of God

Exodus 34:5-7 (New International Version)

Then the LORD came down in the cloud and stood there with him and proclaimed his name, the LORD. And he passed in front of Moses, proclaiming, "The LORD, the LORD, the compassionate and gracious God, slow to anger, abounding in love and faithfulness, maintaining love to thousands, and forgiving wickedness, rebellion and sin…

In this passage, Moses has been communing with God on the mountain. God passes in front of Moses and proclaims His name before him: "The Lord, the Lord." In scripture, a name is filled with meaning about the person. When God says He will proclaim His name to Moses, He means He is revealing who He is. This is who I AM, Moses!

Let's meditate on the character of the Lord. God proclaims that He is filled with compassion. He sees the struggles of His people; He is not removed from their plight. He is a gracious God, made up of kindness. He is slow to anger. He overflows with love. He is faithful to His people, not leaving them alone or abandoned. His love is steadfast for all. His forgiveness is complete and lacking nothing.

Meditate on God's character toward you and your household today. God is compassionate and gracious to you, filled with kindness and love. He is slow to anger and filled with forgiveness. His love for you overflows and is steadfast. He is completely faithful to your household, and He will never abandon you or your children.

1. What have you learned and what do you believe about God's character? What has influenced your belief?

2. How does this scripture compare with your image of God? I pray that you hear Him speak His name before you, and that you come to know His character.

79

Fortress

Psalm 91:1-2, 4, 7 (New International Version)

Whoever dwells in the shelter of the Most High will rest in the shadow of the Almighty. I will say of the LORD, "He is my refuge and my fortress, my God, in whom I trust." ... He will cover you with his feathers, and under his wings you will find refuge; his faithfulness will be your shield and rampart...A thousand may fall at your side, ten thousand at your right hand, but it will not come near you.

This scripture says that when we abide in the shelter of the Living God, we will rest in God's shadow. He will cover us with His Spirit, and we will rest. It is interesting that the next part of the Psalm refers to God being our fortress, our refuge when a thousand fall, when ten thousand fall around us. What are we doing? We are resting in the shadow of God the Almighty One. We are trusting in Him, and He covers us. Covering, resting, refuge, resting, trust. Though a thousand may fall—though ten thousand may fall—when we are covered by God the Almighty, resting in trust, His faithfulness is our protection.

Our refuge is the person of God. It is His covering over us with faithfulness and love when we assume a position of rest and trust. We cannot find refuge in our own strength. Our actions and abilities have a place in the journey, but they are not our fortresses. Our shield and rampart is the faithfulness of the living God. He desires you, He draws you in, and He covers you. Rest in Him.

1. Resting takes practice, faith, and trust. How can you practice this rest under God's covering today?

2. We are leaving our children a legacy, a heritage. Have we taught them by example how to rest under the wings of the Almighty God?

80

When

Luke 23:42-43 (New International Version)

Then he said, "Jesus, remember me when you come into your kingdom." Jesus answered him, "Truly I tell you, today you will be with me in paradise."

I have been meditating on vision and faith these last weeks. I am so struck by this scripture, which tells of the thief being crucified next to Jesus. In the past, when I have studied this verse, it has been discussed as an example of how people can get into heaven "at the last minute" even though they have done wrong things in their life. But, this morning, I realized how much faith was displayed in the thief's words. I can't think of faith that matched this at the cross! He essentially not only recognized the identity of Jesus as the Messiah, but he stated, "Lord, remember me WHEN You come into Your kingdom." WOW. He was the only one at the crucifixion who saw beyond the cross and knew that Jesus would still come into His kingdom! He saw beyond the visible. He was the only one at the cross who said, "WHEN you come into your kingdom." He looked into the eyes of a dying man, and he saw beyond the visible. He saw beyond that moment. He knew that Jesus was Messiah AND that He would come into His kingdom. That is great faith.

God, we pray for GREAT vision and faith. We need to see beyond our current circumstances, beyond what we see with our eyes, beyond what our mind is thinking about "reality," loss and grief. We pray with supernatural faith, knowing that even when things in the natural look final, devastating, and unchangeable...GOOD IS COMING. GOD IS WITH US. NOTHING IS LOST! We speak these truths over our children and our households today.

1. Ask God to give you vision and faith today to see beyond your moment and circumstance. Pray that God will reveal what is unseen and yet most real.

2. Meditate on this scripture today. Can you picture yourself looking at Jesus's face and into His kingdom?

81

He Who Loves

1 John 4:7-8 (Amplified Bible)

Beloved, let us love one another, for love is (springs) from God; and he who loves {his fellowmen} is begotten (born) of God and is coming {progressively} to know and understand God {to perceive and recognize and get a better and clearer knowledge of Him}. He who does not love has not become acquainted with God {does not and never did know Him}, for God is love.

Love is so central to who God is and how He interacts with all people. It is so important to know God inside and out, into the deep, the now, and the forever. If we do not love, this means we do not know God. We have never known Him. Love springs from God, gushes forth, never-ending and ever flowing. The more we know God, the more we understand His deep love for us, for our children, and for all those whose lives we touch on a daily basis.

How we treat others is important; it reflects how deeply we know and understand God. The person you interacted with yesterday is the beloved of God. The one you came in contact with five minutes ago is pursued by God and loved deeply into eternity. God desires intimate connection with the person you are meeting with later this afternoon. God speaks his name.

He wants to be with her forever. The more deeply we know God, the more we honor those around us, and the more completely and clearly we see their God-given identity and call it forth. The more we know love, the more we see each individual as the beloved, the desired, and the pursued. We seek to be a blessing to all around us, never shaming or demeaning others, but lifting them up with the love that emanates from God.

1. Is it easy or difficult to view yourself as God's beloved? In what ways is it easy or difficult to view others as His beloved?

2. Who can you reach out to today with love and honor? Are there people involved in your child's care who need to feel your honor and know that they are loved?

82

Glimpses

1 Chronicles 17:16-17 (The Message)

King David went in, took his place before God, and prayed: Who am I, my Master God, and what is my family, that you have brought me to this place in life? But that's nothing compared to what's coming, for you've also spoken of my family far into the future, given me a glimpse into tomorrow and looked on me, Master God, as a Somebody.

This passage makes me smile. How human David's heart is as he shares his awe of God. He stands in awe of a God who is personal, intimate, and works for the good of His people. This God calls us into life with purpose and destiny. His words and plans propel us into the future. His gaze is on us; He sees us and knows us like no other. How incredible that we have a God who speaks over our families far into the future. Not only does God propel us forward with good purpose, but He also gives us glimpses into tomorrow. He looks on us and tells us who we are.

I pray over you right now, reader. I pray that you will have glimpses into the tomorrow of God. I pray that you will hear what He speaks over you, your children, and your family. I pray that His words over your future will fill you with faith, confidence, and awe. May you know who you are, truly, deeply, and eternally.

1. Have you heard God's heartbeat over your family? Pray that God will speak to you about His heart for your household. Pray that you will hear and see His words of purpose concerning the future of your family.

2. Journal about a time when you heard God speak of your present or future. Did you see a glimpse of His plan? How did your feelings relate to David's feelings of awe?

83

Plant a Garden

Jeremiah 29:5-7 (The Message)

Build houses and make yourselves at home. Put in gardens and eat what grows in that country. Marry and have children. Encourage your children to marry and have children so that you'll thrive in that country and not waste away. Make yourselves at home there and work for the country's welfare. Pray for Babylon's well-being. If things go well for Babylon, things will go well for you.

In this scripture, Jeremiah is speaking to a large group of Jewish exiles who were forcibly taken captive and brought to Babylon. Not only were they taken captive from their homes and forced to live in a foreign land as exiles; they were taken from the Temple. The Temple was not just a "church" building for the Jewish people. This was the physical dwelling place of God Almighty. They were physically taken from the actual home of the manifest Presence of their God. They were homesick and longed to return to their land.

Here Jeremiah encourages these grieving people to not look backward and mourn. These exiles are encouraged to build houses and plant gardens. He instructs them to make themselves at home and to pray for the country's welfare "so that you'll thrive in that country and not waste away." God knows there will be a time for returning to their own land, but in the season of exile, He wants them to thrive by building houses, planting gardens, and praying for Babylon's welfare.

There are times that we may feel like captives in a foreign land. We may be a people in mourning for the past who look back and grieve for what has been lost. We may be longing for a different time and place. Maybe we should take Jeremiah's advice. Let's look to God and say, "I pray for a different season. But while I'm here, I will build a house and plant a garden. I will pray for blessing and favor in this land that my household may prosper and all will go well for us."

1. In what way are you feeling stuck where you don't want to be? How can you pray for blessing within your current place while still praying for the season to end?

2. Think of practical ways to pray in your situation. You may decide to pray for your workplace, your city, or your church. You may pray for the welfare of your child's medical team or school staff. Rather than looking back to mourn, plant a garden and pray over your "Babylon" today.

84

Weight of Glory

2 Corinthians 4:16-17 (Amplified Bible)

Therefore we do not become discouraged (utterly spiritless, exhausted, and wearied out through fear). Though our outer man is {progressively} decaying and wasting away, yet our inner self is being {progressively} renewed day after day. For our light, momentary affliction (this slight distress of the passing hour) is ever more and more abundantly preparing and producing and achieving for us an everlasting weight of glory {beyond all measure, excessively surpassing all comparisons and all calculations, a vast and transcendent glory and blessedness never to cease!}.

Sometimes the circumstances we are in can feel weighty. The load can feel difficult to carry at times. It is easy to feel that we are becoming increasingly bowed down. In Corinthians, Paul talks about how he wards off discouragement, exhaustion, and weariness caused by fear. He says even in the midst of affliction, he knows we are renewed inside, day after day. The distress of this season is passing, but is preparing and producing for us an "everlasting weight of glory." The weight of glory! It feels weighty to replace the load of affliction. It is the glory that is "beyond all measure, excessively surpassing all comparisons and all calculations, a vast and transcendent glory and blessedness never to cease!"

I pray for you right now, reader. I pray that the weight of glory that transcends all momentary afflictions will settle over your household and cover you. May your children know what it is to be renewed day after day on the inside, even when their outsides feel the distress of the hour. I pray that the realization of how huge and transcendent the glory of God is will chase away discouragement and lighten your heart!

1. What things contribute to the season of trouble for you, your children, or your household?

2. In what ways have you experienced the weight of glory? How has this lightened your heart and protected you from fear and discouragement?

85

FEAST

PSALM 23:5 (CONTEMPORARY ENGLISH VERSION)

You treat me to a feast, while my enemies watch. You honor me as your guest, and you fill my cup until it overflows.

During difficult seasons of life, it is so encouraging to know that God prepares a feast for us! There are times that I feel so stretched and spread thin. I sometimes feel that I am in survival mode every day, warring against things that come against us, and searching for solutions and respite. Not only does God offer us rest, but He also offers us a feast, and as we are feasting, our enemies watch. They sit on the sidelines while God says, "Do you want the soup or the salad?" All the powers of darkness watch as God puts His wonderful mercy, grace, and love for us on display. We are fed, warmed, and protected by the love of the most high God. How filling, how comforting—what a feast!

Let His love feed you today. I pray over you and your household. May you and your children know that you are the beloved of God. May your soul rejoice and shout, "You love me so much, God! My cup overflows." May your children be filled with the love of God for them. I pray that you and your children will feast at God's banqueting table today!

1. In what ways can you meditate on the feast today? I invite you to taste and see that the Lord is good.

2. How can you invite your children to know the God of the feast?

86

RESOURCES

DEUTERONOMY 8:4 (AMPLIFIED BIBLE)

Your clothing did not become old upon you nor did your feet swell these forty years.

When you are raising a child with special needs, you are likely to feel the pressure of resources and provision, wondering if there will be enough. Will there be enough finances, energy, patience, assistance, or wisdom? I like this verse from Deuteronomy. Moses is reminding the Israelites about God's provision in the desert. There were times when God provided resources "out of thin air," such as manna, water, and meat. God also provided for their needs by supernaturally extending the life of their resources. Throughout forty years, their clothing never became old, never wore out, or needed to be replaced. Their bodies didn't show the expected wear and tear of walking miles and miles through the desert. The expected blisters and swelling never materialized. God extended their resources to meet their needs.

I pray for your household right now, reader. I pray that the God of the desert journey will not only provide new things that you need on your journey, but will supernaturally extend the life of what you already have. I pray that your current resources won't need to be replaced and won't show the expected wear and tear. May God cover you with His provision in ways that you can't explain in the natural!

1. I invite you to watch for ways in which God meets your needs by extending resources in unexplained and unexpected ways.

2. I pray that this provision from God will be a witness to you and your children about God's heart and His supernatural ways. I encourage you to journal about this part of your journey with God.

87

TREASURE

MATTHEW 25:14-18 (CONTEMPORARY ENGLISH VERSION)

The kingdom is also like what happened when a man went away and put his three servants in charge of all he owned. The man knew what each servant could do. So he handed five thousand coins to the first servant, two thousand to the second, and one thousand to the third. Then he left the country. As soon as the man had gone, the servant with the five thousand coins used them to earn five thousand more. The servant who had two thousand coins did the same with his money and earned two thousand more. But the servant with one thousand coins dug a hole and hid his master's money in the ground.

Consider this. You are entrusted with a treasure of great value. The treasure belongs to the King, and He has left it in your keeping for this season. The treasure is a person. You are married to the King's own son or daughter. Your child is a prince of God, a princess of the highest Kingdom. As the parable above teaches, when the King leaves a treasure in our keeping, He wants to see it increase. He wants to see abundance bubbling over and bursting through.

Pray about this today. How have you invested in the treasures in your life? Has each person entrusted to you increased in your keeping? Have you spoken life, identity, courage, faith, and purpose into their lives? Are they more alive in Spirit glory than they were before they were entrusted to you, or have they become smaller, buried, and more closed and silent? The Kingdom is always about increase, advance, and abundance. There is no poverty or smallness there. Let's make sure that the people we are entrusted with are increasing in glory-goodness, identity, and life while they are in our keeping.

1. Who has been entrusted to your care? Is this person stuck in smallness right now?

2. How can you breathe increase and life over them?

88

ROADS

ISAIAH 30:21 (CONTEMPORARY ENGLISH VERSION)

Whether you turn to the right or to the left, you will hear a voice saying, "This is the road! Now follow it."

Wisdom, I invite you to come, and tell me of eternal things and present things. Cover me and breathe life into me. This scripture grounds me whenever I feel blown about in the winds of confusion. One of the challenges of raising a child with extraordinary needs is that everyone has plenty of advice. If I am the good parent I want to be, which road will I choose for treatment, intervention, and support? What will I chase after and what will I let go? What will I sacrifice for, and when will I rest? What will I work for, and what will I lay at your feet, God, trusting in your intervention and goodness? When will I keep silent, and when will I speak? What will I say?

God, we need your true, rooting wisdom. We need to see and know and hear from your Spirit. Holy Spirit, come and whisper in our ears! Tell us when to turn and when to stay straight on the path. Come dwell in us and whisper truth to our spirits. In sleeping and waking, keep us filled with your revelations. Help us to see.

1. God speaks. He communicates with His people. What has God whispered to your spirit recently? Did you write it down and meditate on it? Do you hold it dear?

2. In what area of parenting do you need insight and understanding? Ask God for this wisdom today, and listen to what He says next. Journal about what you hear. Trust Him to communicate with your open ears.

89

Goodness

Exodus 33:18-19 (New International Version)

Then Moses said, "Now show me your glory." And the LORD said, "I will cause all my goodness to pass in front of you, and I will proclaim my name, the LORD, in your presence."

In Exodus 3, Moses approached the burning bush. God identified Himself, and Moses hid his face because he was afraid to look at God. Then by Exodus 33, Moses met with the Lord, asking for more of Him, wanting to see His glory. I love the cry of his heart! Show me your glory God; show me your glory! I want to see you. I want to know you. More God, More! And God answered the cry of his heart. God said, "I will cause all my goodness to pass in front of you, and I will proclaim my name, the LORD, in your presence."

God's glory is His goodness. Show me all your glory God! Yes, says the Lord; I will show you all my goodness and proclaim my name to you! God tells us that His very essence, His presence, His character, His name, His glory *is* His goodness. His goodness shines all around! As God's goodness passed before Moses, he stood in the cleft of a rock with God's hand covering him. And still the glory of God was so bright that Moses's face shone as he came down the mountain to the people. This time, instead of Moses hiding from God's face, the Jewish people are afraid to approach Moses because his countenance shone with God's glory-goodness! Moses covered his face with a veil when he stood before the people, but he removed the veil whenever he approached God.

1. God's glory is His goodness. Where is your heart? Do you want to approach the glory or hide from it?

2. Do you trust God's goodness? Do you spend enough time in the presence of God's glory-goodness that your countenance shines?

90

Waiting

Isaiah 64:4 (The Message)

Since before time began no one has ever imagined, No ear heard, no eye seen, a God like you who works for those who wait for him.

Waiting is difficult. Some seasons may involve more waiting than others. I would rather be sowing or reaping than waiting. When I wait, rest, or pause, I tend to feel anxious or restless. Activity helps calm my fears. It helps me feel as if I am fixing something, moving forward, making things better. Can I wait on God?

I remember going through a season of waiting some years ago. It was a "growth experience." Don't you love those? In reality, it was very good for me. I realized that waiting could be worship. Don't get me wrong; waiting can also come out of fear, inertia, or unbelief. However, for me, that season was about my ability to wait in complete trust and faith in God—to live in ambiguity within a life that was unfixed and unsettled, and to be able to be incomplete and undone for a season.

Waiting was worship for me. It was the sweet incense of trust and faith in a good God. As you wait on God, believe that He is working for you! The wonderful things that God does for you while you wait are unimaginable.

1. When have you experienced a season of waiting? What are you waiting for now?

2. Do you find it easier to be active or to wait? How do you demonstrate faith and trust in God as He works for you?

91

BOUNTY

PSALM 65:11 (NEW INTERNATIONAL VERSION)

You crown the year with your bounty, and your carts overflow with abundance.

We have an abundant God. He overflows with goodness and provision. Everything He does is fruitful, producing plenty. Even the hard pathways, where nothing can take root and grow in the natural, will overflow with bountiful harvest. What hard pathways are you encountering this season? Do you feel that you lack in any aspect of your life?

I pray abundance into every hard pathway of your life. I speak this scripture over you and your children. God will crown your year with bounty. I pray for breakthrough in all areas that have you bound or struggling. Let's pray together for breakthrough in the areas of health, relationships, identity, finances, endurance, ministry, property, and wisdom. The list goes on and on, and so does God's provision. May He reign and rain over your lives this year, even today.

1. Identify two areas of life that are a hard path for you or your child this season.

2. Pray this scripture over those areas this month. I join you in praying for fruitfulness and breakthrough! Let's never stop crying out to heaven for abundance to be released in every area of need.

92

God Wins

Judges 7:4, 7 (Contemporary English Version)

"Gideon," the LORD said, "you still have too many soldiers. Take them down to the spring and I'll test them. I'll tell you which ones can go along with you and which ones must go back home." ...The LORD said, "Gideon, your army will be made up of everyone who lapped the water from their hands. Send the others home. I'm going to rescue Israel by helping you and your army of three hundred defeat the Midianites."

In this passage, Gideon is gathering an army in response to God's call. Gideon will lead the army and defeat the enemy through the Lord's power. But God tells Gideon that he has too many soldiers to win the victory. How can this be possible? Gideon started out with thirty-two thousand men, and in the end, the Lord whittled down the number to three hundred. The enemy was estimated to include hundreds of thousands of soldiers, and scriptures say that the number of camels alone was harder to count than grains of sand on a beach. But God said, "I'm going to rescue Israel by helping you and your army of three hundred defeat the Midianites." They would go in the presence and power of the Lord, three hundred to defeat a massive enemy.

This passage underscores that God doesn't need things stacked in His direction in order win victory. He doesn't look for situations that appear "winnable." He doesn't search out situations that lean toward victory, nor does He need people that can defeat the enemy by their own strength. God wins in every circumstance. Victory, freedom, and wholeness are His in all situations. The numbers of the enemy are of no consequence. The experience and resources of the enemy add up to nothing in God's presence. The track record of the opposing army means nothing. God is God. He wins victory in every situation.

1. In what situations do you feel outnumbered or "out-gunned?" Do you realize that this is of no consequence in God's kingdom?

2. Victories are won through God's power and presence. In what area of your child's life are you looking for breakthrough? How can you immerse yourself in God's presence to prepare for battle?

93

NOTHING IS LOST

ACTS 3:20-21 (NEW INTERNATIONAL VERSION)

...and that he may send the Messiah, who has been appointed for you—even Jesus. Heaven must receive him until the time comes for God to restore everything, as he promised long ago through his holy prophets.

We have a God who restores, rebuilds, and makes all things new. The theme of restoration is told and retold all throughout scripture. I sometimes wake up in the night with something running through my head that I need to write down in my journal. One night, I woke up hearing this: Nothing is lost in Christ. In Christ, everything is gain, and outside of Christ, everything is loss.

In the scripture, Jesus described Satan as a thief. John 10:10 (NIV) says, "The thief comes only to steal and kill and destroy." As a parent of a child with extraordinary needs, it is easy to feel a sense of loss, and to feel that something has been stolen from you and your family. You may notice that your child misses out on things that other kids enjoy without effort. You may feel that your connection with your child and/or your spouse is not what you wish it could be. You may say that the dreams you had for your family seem far away.

I don't diminish at all the sense of loss and grief that can occur in this context. But when I woke up that night, I felt like God was speaking within my head. I was reminded that we have an eternal God who is a God of restoration. He holds everything in His eternal hands. Nothing runs through His fingers. There is no lack, no surprise, and no loss in Him. All things are held by Him for the day of restoration. I don't know what that will look like or when it will happen, but as a matter of faith, I declare that in Christ, all things will be restored!

1. How is the theme of restoration developed in the lives of people recorded in scripture (e.g., Abraham, Moses, David, Nehemiah)?

2. In what ways have you witnessed restoration in the lives of people around you?

3. What things in your life feel lost? How can you believe God for restoration in these areas?

94

Agreement

Philippians 2:5 (Contemporary English Version)

Think the same way that Christ Jesus thought.

I remember my husband and I doing a Bible study about ten years ago. Part of the study was talking about how important it is to have the mind of Christ. Our friends from church talked through that, and I'm not sure we ended with much clarity. Does having the mind of Christ mean we should be humble, kind, or generous? What quality does the "mind of Christ" capture, and what does it look like on a day-to-day basis?

Over this past year, I think I've "gotten it," or, I am on the road to getting it! I believe that having the mind of Christ means that I should not have a thought in my head that Christ does not have. I should not think about anything (e.g., my child, my circumstance, my identity, my finances, my health, my future, or my relationships) in a way that is contrary to what God is thinking. That is revolutionary for me, and challenging of course! But it's vital.

When I catch myself thinking, *I'm really alone; no one sees me or knows me*, I need to determine whether that thought agrees or disagrees with what God is thinking and saying. One way to do this is to take the Bible and compare the word of God with my thoughts. When I read Psalm 139:1-2 (You have searched me, LORD, and you know me. You know when I sit and when I rise; you perceive my thoughts from afar—NIV), I need to allow that truth to challenge my thinking that I am unseen and alone. I should not have a thought in my head that God is not thinking. In short, the scripture challenges me to live in agreement with God.

1. Identify three of your thoughts that you believe are in disagreement with God's thoughts.

2. Identify scriptures that contradict each thought. Print out these scriptures and tape them to your bathroom mirror. Speak them aloud every morning and evening for one month.

3. Journal about the impact this exercise has on your thought process and life.

95

Presence

Exodus 33:1-3, 15, 17 (The Message)

God said to Moses, "Now go. Get on your way from here, you and the people you brought up from the land of Egypt. Head for the land which I promised to Abraham, Isaac, and Jacob, saying, 'I will give it to your descendants.' I will send an angel ahead of you and I'll drive out the Canaanites, Amorites, Hittites, Perizzites, Hivites, and Jebusites. It's a land flowing with milk and honey. But I won't be with you in person...Moses said, "If your presence doesn't take the lead here, call this trip off right now...God said to Moses: "All right. Just as you say; this also I will do, for I know you well and you are special to me. I know you by name."

I love this exchange between Moses and God. At this point in the journey, they have met together regularly. There is an intimate, personal, knowing connection between them. But God expresses frustration with the hard hearts of the Israelites that won't let Him in. God says to Moses that He will fulfill His promise to give them the Promised Land. He will also drive out all of their enemies. However, God Himself will not come with them; He will send an angel instead.

That was an interesting choice point, wasn't it? It was a choice between the promise and the Presence, the gift and the Giver. If you were offered the promise without the Presence, which would you choose? Moses chose Presence. He said to God, "If your presence doesn't take the lead here, call this trip off right now."

We have a relational God. He does not come to us in any other way. It is for relationship that He sent His only son, Jesus, to die and rise again, destroying separation forever. Connection and intimacy with God are important. The Presence of God is meant to be everything to you! It needs to fill you up and be your sustenance. I pray that you will hunger and thirst for Presence as much as Moses did. When you hunger and thirst for Him, you will be filled up to overflowing with His living Spirit!

1. Are you on a journey with God? Is your focus on destination or relationship?

2. How can you foster more intimacy in your relationship with God today?

96

THE COMING KING

ISAIAH 40:3-5 (AMPLIFIED BIBLE)

A voice of one who cries: Prepare in the wilderness the way of the Lord {clear away the obstacles}; make straight and smooth in the desert a highway for our God! Every valley shall be lifted and filled up, and every mountain and hill shall be made low; and the crooked and uneven shall be made straight and level, and the rough places a plain. And the glory (majesty and splendor) of the Lord shall be revealed, and all flesh shall see it together...

When you are parenting children who have struggles and specific needs, there seem to be many obstacles, rough places, and uneven paths. The wilderness can seem foreboding. In the fortieth chapter, Isaiah prophesies about John the Baptist, a voice crying out in the wilderness (see Mark 1:3). John cried out, preparing the way for Jesus to enter into His ministry.

In those days, if a king from an outlying country were coming to your kingdom, you would send out workers to make a smooth road for the king to enter your domain. The path would be made smooth, straight, and level. This was a way of preparing for the king, ushering him into your area. All obstacles and all rough places must go! They must give way to the coming king!

I pray over your home and your children, reader! I pray that your King will be ushered into your life in a manifest and glorious way. I speak to the obstacles in your life, that they must give way. I speak over your body, mind, and spirit; I pray that the path of your King will be made smooth, straight, and level. The King is coming to bring His Kingdom into your life. May He usher in health, shalom, and grace.

1. What obstacle is evident in your life today? Is it an issue of the heart, the body, the mind, or the spirit? I pray with you that the rough place will be made smooth, and the King will be ushered into that very place!

2. In what ways can you prepare the path for the King and usher in His Kingdom? In what ways do you need God to move on your behalf and a community to help in this work?

97

Design and Purpose

Ephesians 1:11-12 (The Message)

It's in Christ that we find out who we are and what we are living for. Long before we first heard of Christ and got our hopes up, he had his eye on us, had designs on us for glorious living, part of the overall purpose he is working out in everything and everyone.

What are we here for? What are we living for? God created us with design and purpose. When we are living in Christ, we find out who we are. We find out who we are by finding out who He is intimately through experiential knowledge gathered day-by-day over years and seasons. It is an unfolding story of who He is and who we are in Him. We have been created and called for glorious living. We are called into glory, goodness, and happiness. We are part of God's overall purpose for everyone. God speaks identity and destiny over each of us, and when we are all living out our purpose in Christ, we are a blessing to others. People, communities, and nations are blessed all around us.

God, I pray for the mothers and fathers reading these devotions. I pray for their children and their households. Speak over their lives, God. Let them see with unfolding clarity the gift they are to those around them, and the powerhouse they are in

Christ. Help them to know and understand that none of their struggles in the natural detracts from their glorious identity in Christ! Their design, purpose, destiny, and identity in Christ is always glory and goodness. Show them how to impact their world for good!

1. What is your identity? What are your children called to do? Listen to the heartbeat of God and believe.

2. Join God in speaking destiny over your children. Believe that no struggle in this world will detract one minutia from the eternal impact of their lives in the kingdom! Believe.

98

Promises

Joshua 21:45 (New International Version)

Not one of all the LORD's good promises to Israel failed; every one was fulfilled.

God's faithfulness is unchangeable and enduring. The book of Joshua describes God's faithfulness to the Israelites as they entered the Promised Land. I love this verse. Read it aloud with me. *Not one of all the Lord's good promises to Israel failed; every one was fulfilled.* Say it again. Print it out and tape it on your refrigerator. No a single one of God's good promises failed.

God is a faithful God. He is faithful to you. He will not let you down or abandon you. Every one of His promises will be fulfilled; they will all come to pass. Sometimes, this feels true, striking, and beautiful. Other times, this verse feels far off and false. I pray that God will speak to you today about His promises to you and your children. I pray He will talk to you about your circumstances. Hear God's voice speaking to you today about His eternal truth, His process, and His ways. I encourage you to hold onto faith for His promises. They will all be fulfilled, nothing lacking and nothing lost.

1. Have you heard God's voice speaking to you about His promises for your family? What has He promised?

2. Spend some quiet time in prayer today, asking the Spirit to surround you with the truth about the faithfulness of God.

99

Dwelling God

Ezekiel 48:35 (The Message)

The four sides of the city measure to a total of nearly six miles. From now on the name of the city will be Yahweh-Shammah: "God-Is-There."

This scripture reveals one of the names of God given to us in scripture, Yahweh-Shammah. It is the last name of God revealed through the Old Testament prophets. In the context of Ezekiel, the name was revealed to Israel when the people were returning to their land after a seventy-year captivity in Babylon. The name spoke promise; it spoke of the restoration of Jerusalem. God tells Ezekiel that the very land itself will be called "God is There." This name was a revelation to the people and a reassurance to them that their God is a God that dwells near. He abides with them as part of His very nature.

One thing I love about God is that He tells His story again and again. In Ezekiel, He tells the people He will dwell in their land. We also see the Abiding God in the Person of Jesus who came to the land and dwelt among the people. Following the death and resurrection of Christ, all believers can personally experience this Dwelling-God inside their very person. We are now the land in which God dwells; we are His temple. God is with us, He is among us, and He is in us. What a God of closeness we have! No matter what your feelings, no matter what your circumstances, God is with you. His very character and fundamental nature is that He is an abiding and dwelling God, and He chooses to abide with and in you.

1. Meditate on the nature of God as Yahweh-Shammah today. What does this mean for you and your family?

2. Decide not to rely on your feelings and circumstances, but rather to embrace the covenant-keeping God who wants above all to be near to you. In what practical ways can you and your children embrace the God who is with you? How might that look on a daily basis?

100

The Answer

Judges 7:12 (Contemporary English Version)

The camp was huge. The Midianites, Amalekites, and other eastern nations covered the valley like a swarm of locusts. And it would be easier to count the grains of sand on a beach than to count their camels.

How would you describe the opposition in your life right now? Do you feel outnumbered? In Judges 7, Gideon is leading a small army against a large, experienced, and equipped enemy. He looks out over the camp and sees that the enemy number more than the grains of sand on a beach—they cover the horizon and beyond. The camp, the enemy, the weapons, and the camels are like grains of sand. This is the opposition Gideon must face.

Many of us are battling an enemy today and facing oppositions too numerous and powerful to number. There is a truth we must know and understand deeply within in our very being. We must know that the answer is in God, not in the problem. The victory is in the Presence, not in the opposition. Victory, freedom, and breakthrough are won with God's Presence, not by analyzing the enemy, counting the camels, and surveying the landscape. Enter into His Presence today and every day. Lie still in His Presence. Rest in His presence. Be surrounded by Him today. He is the answer. The solution to every problem is in Him and through Him, always, forever, and completely.

1. Does surveying the problems in your life bring you freedom? In what ways has dwelling on the problems been counterproductive?

2. What is the biggest challenge to resting in the Presence of God daily? What personal experiences of victory and freedom have you known in His Presence?

101

God's Word

Psalm 119:105 (New International Version)

Your word is a lamp for my feet, a light on my path.

Everything that God is doing in your life and in the life of your child is for freedom, for good, and for life. However, sometimes the journey is confusing and takes you beyond the known into the unexpected and unplanned. It is likely that God has led you into territory with no map and only His voice for guidance. His Word lights your way. His voice is your light and your direction.

This scripture speaks to me about the journey. As I meditate on this verse, I realize that sometimes I find that I have been given a lamp only on my feet to guide me moment by moment. At other times, God's Word enlightens my whole path. I can see more of the big picture. I can see some direction ahead, the winding of the road, the horizon. I have been in both places, both seasons. I am learning to dwell in either reality. Each involves God's voice, light, steps, direction, and listening.

1. Think about your journey with God and with your children. Can you recognize the different seasons? Which are you in today?

2. What is your comfort level with your journey? Do you prefer light on your feet or your path? Can you learn to feel grounded in either season with God?

102

Hope and Grief

2 Kings 4:28 (New International Version)

"Did I ask you for a son, my lord?" she said. "Didn't I tell you, 'Don't raise my hopes'?"

This chapter relates the story of Elisha and the Shunammite woman. The woman recognized Elisha as a man of God. She and her husband made a small room on the roof of their house for Elisha. Whenever he came through their town, Elisha stayed with them. The woman had been unable to have a child. Elisha prophesied that she would have a child, and the next year she gave birth to a son. One day, when the child was old enough, he went out to the fields to see his father. He complained of head pain, was taken to his mother, and died in her lap. The Shunammite woman laid her son on Elisha's bed. She ran out to Elisha and told him what happened. In verse 28, she describes her range of emotions, putting into words the pain of receiving something only to lose it ("Didn't I tell you, 'Don't raise my hopes?'").

Many of us can relate to the woman's reaction. We understand the roller coaster of emotions when we lack something, gain something, only to lose it again. Praying for breakthrough intensifies our awareness of our need for breakthrough. As we intercede, we hope and grieve at the same time.

We are not allowed the "luxury" of living life with our emotions turned off. We feel the risk involved in a life of faith.

The story ends as Elisha returns to the home to pray over the boy. The boy is resurrected back to life. This is the culmination of our story as believers as well. We ultimately know and experience the God of restoration, life, and resurrection. In the end, we have lost nothing in God.

1. Have you experienced the risk of faith? Have your fears of loss kept you from believing for the impossible?

2. Can you commit to present your every need, desire, and dream to the God of resurrection and life?

103

Keep Looking

1 Kings 18:41-45 (The Message)

Elijah said to Ahab, "Up on your feet! Eat and drink—celebrate! Rain is on the way; I hear it coming." Ahab did it: got up and ate and drank. Meanwhile, Elijah climbed to the top of Carmel, bowed deeply in prayer, his face between his knees. Then he said to his young servant, "On your feet now! Look toward the sea." He went, looked, and reported back, "I don't see a thing." "Keep looking," said Elijah, "seven times if necessary." And sure enough, the seventh time he said, "Oh yes, a cloud! But very small, no bigger than someone's hand, rising out of the sea."

"Quickly then, on your way. Tell Ahab, 'Saddle up and get down from the mountain before the rain stops you.'" Things happened fast. The sky grew black with wind-driven clouds, and then a huge cloudburst of rain...

This story takes place at the end of a severe famine in the land resulting from three years of no rain. At the beginning of this chapter, God tells Elijah that the rain is coming. It's as good as falling and soaking right now. It's a done deal, although the land is still dry. Things in the heavens were already changed; God's word had been sent out to break through the natural. Elijah, knowing what God said, knowing that breakthrough was coming, told the king to eat and celebrate. He called for a feast, not because the breakthrough had come, but because the breakthrough was coming. He could hear it in the atmosphere, echoing from God's voice. The feast was an act of faith, faith that God's word was true and complete, even before the natural had changed.

So the king ate and drank. Meanwhile, Elijah went to the top of the mountain to pray in the word. He bowed deeply in prayer to join his voice with God's voice, and to call in the victory, the precious soaking that God was speaking into the atmosphere. He sent his servant to look for some sign of breakthrough visible in the natural. Perhaps there were storm clouds rolling in over the water? But, no, six times over there was nothing. Prayer and more prayer, watching and watching, but nothing came until the seventh time. Seven is the scriptural number of completion, perfection, and rest. This time, there was a small cloud far off in the distance, a small sign the size of a man's fist. That was it. That was all that was needed! He warned the king to hurry down the mountain, before the rain stopped him! And, indeed, the drenching rains came and refreshed the earth!

1. What in your life feels like drought and famine? What breakthrough are you praying for? Speak it out now.

2. What is God saying to bring breakthrough and victory into your situation? Is He encouraging you to feast? Can you hear the rain coming? Can you see a cloud the size of a man's hand? Pray it in and watch for it; get ready to hitch up your robes and run down the mountain!

104

CHILD OF THE KING

ROMANS 8:15 (NEW INTERNATIONAL VERSION)

The Spirit you received does not make you slaves, so that you live in fear again; rather, the Spirit you received brought about your adoption to sonship. And by him we cry, "Abba, Father."

When we invite God into our lives, we receive His Spirit. What does that mean? Paul describes one of the implications here when he writes to Roman believers. He is making sure that they understand that God's Spirit does not bind them up and cause them to be slaves to fear. There is a spirit that does that, but it is not from God. Anyone who has experienced the presence of persistent, hounding fear that leaves you bound up and trapped (e.g., for your kids, your finances, your health), has experienced the spirit of fear (see also 2 Timothy 1:7). Rather, God's Spirit transforms us into full children of God. He is not only our Lord, but also our Abba, which is like saying "Daddy" in Aramaic.

We need to fully realize that once we have invited God's spirit into our lives, we are no longer orphans. Sometimes I hear myself praying "like an orphan" with the mentality of someone who is in poverty. This is "praying out of poverty," and it is in contrast to praying out of my identity in Christ!

I am not an orphan; I am a child of the King. My Daddy has unlimited resources, and I am His beloved and heir (see Ephesians 3:6 and Romans 8:17). Fear, poverty, lack, and an orphan-spirit all go together. When I pray, I need to pray from my identity; I am a daughter of the King!

---

1. Have you ever felt trapped by a spirit of fear? Can you think of a time when you prayed like an orphan? Do you know that this was not from God?

2. What would it mean for you to change the mentality your prayer? How can you pray from a position of intimacy rather than fear? How can you pray to your Daddy-God, the King with unlimited resources?

105

Provision

Genesis 22:13-14 (The Message)

Abraham looked up. He saw a ram caught by its horns in the thicket. Abraham took the ram and sacrificed it as a burnt offering instead of his son. Abraham named that place God-Yireh (God-Sees-to-It). That's where we get the saying, "On the mountain of God, he sees to it."

Throughout the scripture, when God interacts with His people, He reveals who He is in various ways. One way that He reveals His identity is through His "names." In the Bible, a person's name was a revelation about his/her character and identity. There are many names of God revealed in the scripture, and whole books have been written just on this subject. In Genesis 22, there is the name YHVH Yireh, which is often translated "I AM your provider" or "The LORD Who Sees and Provides." In this passage, God is the One Who Provides an alternate sacrifice, and Isaac is saved. It is an early image and revelation of God's plan to send Jesus as the Lamb of God to become our alternate sacrifice to save us.

We all find ourselves in various situations and circumstances right now. I invite you to ask God what He wants to be for you right now, today, in your current circumstance. Do you need provision? The only way to meet the

God of Provision is to go through a season where you are in need of provision. Then you will meet Him. This is who God is. He is a God of providing.He is your God and your Provision. He is yours!

1. What are your needs today? Make a list the primary needs in your household. Think about your needs, the needs of your family, your children, and your household. Ask God for what you need.

2. May you encounter the God of Provision in this season. I pray that today He will become the provision you need right now. May you encounter His abundance, His caring, and His provision for all your needs.

106

IMPACT

PROVERBS 18:21 (AMPLIFIED BIBLE)

Death and life are in the power of the tongue, and they who indulge in it shall eat the fruit of it {for death or life}.

God has given us power. The words that we speak are powerful. When we speak over people's lives, we speak with impact! When we speak about our circumstances, our future, our abilities, our children, all of these words are living and force-filled. We have the power to free people or hold them bound. We are able to bless others and fill them with courage, or to cover them with negative impact. We have the power to speak significance and purpose into our children and our neighbors. All of these things are in the power of the tongue. We speak and there is real impact!

I pray that you will be a blessing to your children by the words that you speak into their lives. I encourage you to listen to God and speak the same thing He is speaking. You will be a giver of freedom, blessing, mercy, courage, and destiny. You will be a part of calling into being things that are not yet in existence! Your prayers and declarations will make a difference for good! Death and life are in the power of your tongue. Choose life!

1. In what ways have others spoken over your life, your identity, and your future? Has there been power in their words, for life or for death?

2. Do you realize the mighty impact of your words? How can you speak life into your household, your future, and your children?

107

Hidden Things

Jeremiah 33:3 (Amplified Bible)

Call to Me and I will answer you and show you great and mighty things, fenced in and hidden, which you do not know (do not distinguish and recognize, have knowledge of and understand).

I remember the day I discovered this verse tucked away in Jeremiah. It was as if the verse itself was hiding! And here in this hidden verse, God invites us to call on Him, to show us hidden things!

We call to you God, and you answer us! This is part of the Divine exchange, the intimate sharing between you and me—the knowing and being known. I call on you, and you answer me! You are filled with great and mighty things that are not seen, heard, or known without you. You have fenced some things in; you have hidden them in the deep places. Yet, you invite me in to seek them and find them with you.

As a parent, I frequently come to the realization that I need wisdom and knowledge that I don't have. I must search it out, and here is my God, inviting me to call on Him. He invites me into His Presence where He will show me great and mighty things—hidden things that I do not know. *Call me in God! I want to enter into your Presence. I want to see and know and be with*

You in the deep places with the hidden things! Expand my understanding God. Help me know what I don't know.

1. Wow! We have a God who wants to be known. We have a God who wants to show us hidden things in His Presence! I invite you to call on Him today. Pray Jeremiah 33:3, and know that God will answer you and show you hidden things.

2. I pray for you, reader, that God will show you things in the deep places that will change your life, enrich your relationships, and bring your child into health and peace. Be blessed by this verse today.

108

Choose the Best

Luke 10:38-42 (Contemporary English Version)

The Lord and his disciples were traveling along and came to a village. When they got there, a woman named Martha welcomed him into her home. She had a sister named Mary, who sat down in front of the Lord and was listening to what he said. Martha was worried about all that had to be done. Finally, she went to Jesus and said, "Lord, doesn't it bother you that my sister has left me to do all the work by myself? Tell her to come and help me!" The Lord answered, "Martha, Martha! You are worried and upset about so many things, but only one thing is necessary. Mary has chosen what is best, and it will not be taken away from her."

I have been transformed by these verses. If left to my own tendencies, I can be very much like Martha. I am responsible and efficient. I see what needs to be done and I do it. I see what needs to be fixed and I problem solve. So many things need doing and fixing, but these verses are so convicting. They reach down for a deeper truth. To lie at the feet of Jesus and soak Him in, to worship and listen, to be in His presence—this posture is where the intimacy of knowing and being known by another is born.

Intimacy, worship, and being in His Presence are what become most transforming in the end. When we assume this posture, we focus on Presence rather than performance. In worship, we focus on thankfulness instead of lack. In this relationship, we know the One who is above all, and we see that, in the end, more comes to those who lay at His feet: more breakthroughs, more wisdom, more strength and courage, and more provision!

1. Close your eyes right now. Tune out the world. Picture yourself lying at Jesus's feet, soaking Him in. Can you hear the melody of His voice? Can you breathe in the incense of His Presence? Let yourself be known by Him.

2. What things have you been able to receive in a position of intimacy and worship that you have not been able to receive through your own striving?

109

ALERT AND ACTIVE

JEREMIAH 1:11-12 (AMPLIFIED BIBLE)

Moreover, the word of the Lord came to me, saying, Jeremiah, what do you see? And I said, I see a branch or shoot of an almond tree {the emblem of alertness and activity, blossoming in late winter}. Then said the Lord to me, you have seen well, for I am alert and active, watching over My word to perform it.

What may seem like an obscure and confusing verse has become beloved by me. There are times that God speaks with symbols and layers of meaning. Things in the world around us can mirror what God is saying. Here, the Lord asks Jeremiah what he sees. Jeremiah looks in the natural and sees the shoot of an almond tree. In Hebrew culture, the almond tree was a symbol of alertness and activity. It blossomed late in the winter when the cold had settled deep and the land was dormant and without fruit. There was much in the natural at that time to suggest inactivity, dormancy, and death. But Jeremiah saw a symbol of God's alertness and activity. The Lord said, "You have seen well, for I am alert and active, watching over My word to perform it."

This is a verse to hold on to when everything in the natural feels cold and dead, without a hint of breakthrough. This is a truth to put your faith in when nothing in the natural supports your faith for a change of season, for an alert and active God, and for fruitfulness and breakthrough. God is active, and He is watching over His Word. Not in complacency and not with idleness, but watching over His Word to perform it, bring it to blossom, calling it forth into the now!

1. Are you watching and waiting for breakthrough that feels impossible in the natural? Meditate on this verse today.

2. God watches over His Word to protect it, brood over it, and bring it into the now. What word are you believing for in the now?

110

Green Hope

Romans 14:13
(The Message)

Oh! May the God of green hope fill you up with joy, fill you up with peace, so that your believing lives, filled with the life-giving energy of the Holy Spirit, will brim over with hope!

I pray, reader, that you will be filled with all hope, the living hope that comes to us from God. When we have hope, we are sure that good things are coming, no matter what. We have faith and we believe that good is coming. It is almost here. No matter what we see, hear, or "know" in the natural, God is coming to bring us His goodness. God is always up to something good on your behalf and on behalf of your children. I wonder what He is doing today? What is He up to in His infinite wisdom and goodness and mercy?

I pray that God will fill you with joy and peace as you believe in His goodness, and that your believing, faith-filled lives will overflow with life and abundant energy from the Spirit! May you brim over with the hope that comes from knowing a good and loving God! He is coming to help you. Good is on its way.

1. Do you have hope for your situation or that of your child? Do you believe that good is coming?

2. In the areas where you feel without hope, are you believing God's truth or the enemy's lie? Is God feeling hopeless about your situation? No! We must agree with Him in all things! We must believe the truth no matter what our circumstances look like in the natural realm. Believe that good is coming! He is coming to you.

111

Live and Proclaim

Psalm 118:17 (New International Version)

I will not die but live, and will proclaim what the LORD has done.

I will not die. I will live and proclaim. The psalmist is most likely speaking of physical death here. When I pray through this psalm, however, I am struck by how this verse speaks to the issue of living or dying within the heart. I have at times felt stuck in my struggle or grieving. At particular times, I have felt dead inside, empty and hollow. Sometimes we have to choose whether to be dead and hollow inside or whether to live, grow, and feel. Choosing can be difficult and monumental at times.

I choose to live in my heart and spirit and to be present and alive, fully feeling. I choose to live in awareness of what is and what is not yet, to feel the tension of living in a world unfixed and undone. I choose to proclaim what the Lord has done, and to speak of God's victories and declare His goodness in the land of the living, even when I am tempted to shut down or turn off my spirit. I choose to live, breathe, feel, and proclaim.

1. Although a person is physically alive, how may he or she choose death in other areas? Have you ever had to choose to live?

2. In what ways can you proclaim goodness during difficult times? Have you ever had to choose between silence and speaking about God's goodness? How has proclaiming His goodness impacted your spirit and the atmosphere around you?

112

Personal Verse

2 Peter 1:2 (Amplified Bible)

May grace (God's favor) and peace (which is perfect well-being, all necessary good, all spiritual prosperity, and freedom from fears and agitating passions and moral conflicts) be multiplied to you in {the full, personal, precise, and correct} knowledge of God and of Jesus our Lord.

I heard a woman once tell how her family had a tradition when she and her siblings were children. Every time someone had a birthday, the rest of the family would choose a Bible verse for that person for the upcoming year. The family would then pray that verse over the person all year long as a blessing, a declaration, and a way to speak over his or her life.

To me, this is just such a verse. Choose a person. Speak this over his or her life today. Joshua, may God's delight and favor pour over you today and always. Emily, I pray that you will know God's peace, His deep calm, which is perfect well-being. Patrick, may you know spiritual prospering in your life and freedom in everything you do. Sarah, may you know release from any fear or agitation. May you know the good and perfect thing to do in each situation. Mark, I pray that all of these things will be multiplied unto you, and that you would know each piece in abundance and overflowing. I pray that in the abundance of this experience, you will know the Lord fully, deeply, and personally.

1. Think about the individuals in your household today. Spend some time this month choosing a verse for each person, including yourself. Write each verse out and declare it over each person daily! Consider making this a family tradition.

2. In what ways have others spoken into your life for good or for bad? Have you experienced the power of others' words? How can you speak blessing over other people consistently and purposefully?

113

Lord All-Powerful

Zechariah 4:6 (Contemporary English Version)

So the angel explained that it was the following message of the LORD to Zerubbabel: I am the LORD All-Powerful. So don't depend on your own power or strength, but on my Spirit.

Who is our God? He is the Lord All-Powerful! He invites us to know and experience His power in our lives. In my own life, I'm fairly efficient and task-oriented. I see something that needs to be done, and I do it. I'm resourceful and good at tackling most obstacles head-on. But anyone who has lived long enough will encounter a problem of sizable magnitude, a mountain, if you will, that cannot be moved. It stands tall and wide, made of solid rock. Our efforts to push, pull, or pummel are to no avail. The mountain remains, and we feel weaker for having tried to move it in the first place.

So God says to Zerubbabel, "I am the LORD All-Powerful. Don't depend on your own power or strength, but rather on my Spirit." As a mother, I have come to know and understand that striving on my part is not a strategy that produces life and fruitfulness. There must be wisdom and balance, a knowing of when to rest and when to work; an understanding of what is a task for God's Spirit and what is a task for me; partnering with God and being able to hear His voice, His heartbeat, and the ability to work and rest in rhythm with Him. I must be able to trust Him with His portion, and to steward my portion well.

1. What do you depend on? Are you a person of striving? Are you one who feels stuck, unable to move, act, or participate in the solution to an obstacle?

2. What does it look like to have such intimacy with God that you can balance work and rest, allowing God to have His portion of the task while you steward your portion well?

114

Released Power

Luke 1:37 (Amplified Bible)

For with God nothing is ever impossible and no word from God shall be without power or impossible of fulfillment.

This is one of my favorite verses. I never noticed it until recent years, but now I meditate on this scripture frequently. The first part of the verse is wonderful and true, but the second part of the verse is what I have come to treasure. Listen to this: "No word from God shall be without power or impossible of fulfillment." Isn't this amazing? God never speaks without releasing power for the promise to be fulfilled. When He declares something and promises something, when He calls forth things that are not yet, the resources and power for fulfillment are released as well. No word from God is without power, nor is it impossible.

I believe that God is always speaking over us. Some of His promises are biblical promises for all His people. Some are individual words to us, to our children, and to our household. Have you heard His voice? What is He saying to you? I encourage you to invite Him to speak into your life. Keep a journal of what you hear. Nothing that God is saying is void of power or resource. When He speaks, He releases everything to unfold in His perfect timing.

1. I want to encourage you to listen today, to meditate on the promises of God, and to believe that there is power and resource behind every word of God.

2. When you hear God speak over your children, speak the same thing. Recite God's promises over them. There is no empty word among them.

115

Friendship

1 Samuel 18:1, 3-4 (The Message)

By the time David had finished reporting to Saul, Jonathan was deeply impressed with David—an immediate bond was forged between them. He became totally committed to David. From that point on he would be David's number-one advocate and friend...Jonathan, out of his deep love for David, made a covenant with him. He formalized it with solemn gifts: his own royal robe and weapons—armor, sword, bow, and belt.

God created us to live connected with others in community and covenant relationships. We are called together to be the body of Christ, each with specific spiritual gifts and roles in the larger community. God created us to need each other. When a family is rallying to support a child with specific needs, the result can be quite isolating for many reasons. These families may find it difficult to connect with others and remain in the bonds of friendship. It may even be difficult to regularly attend church services. They may feel overwhelmed, and at the same time, adrift and alone.

I pray with you, reader, that you will know deep and lasting friendships. I pray that you and your children will have friends that you can play with, rest with, work with, and pray with. I pray that God will bring specific individuals into your life who have Christ living inside of them. I pray that these people will enter into covenant friendships with you, friendships filled with promises and commitment. May they be a part of speaking identity and destiny over your life and each member of your family. I pray that God will speak to them about your needs, and that your friends will be part of your journey with God, calling out solutions to your difficulties and breathing LIFE into your life!

1. Have there been seasons of isolation in your journey? What things in your life right now are working against building community connections within the body of Christ?

2. How can you renew your commitment to seeking relationships and receiving assistance from friends? May God bless you with relationships that are life changing and life giving!

116

FOUNDATIONS

HEBREWS 11:8-10 (AMPLIFIED BIBLE)

{Urged on} by faith Abraham, when he was called, obeyed and went forth to a place which he was destined to receive as an inheritance; and he went, although he did not know or trouble his mind about where he was to go. {Prompted} by faith he dwelt as a temporary resident in the land which was designated in the promise {of God, though he was like a stranger} in a strange country, living in tents with Isaac and Jacob, fellow heirs with him of the same promise. For he was {waiting expectantly and confidently} looking forward to the city which has fixed and firm foundations, whose Architect and Builder is God.

Does faith urge you on? It was by faith that Abraham went forth from the place he had known to the place he did not know—his destined inheritance. He lived in the in-between place while he journeyed with God. He had a promise, but he had not yet reached the destination. He dwelt in tents, a temporary resident in the land that would be his someday. Abraham, Isaac, and Jacob, heirs of the same promise, waited in confident expectation! They waited, anticipating their promised destination—their inheritance—despite it being off in the distance. They looked forward to a city with foundations. They envisioned a time when they had reached the promise and no longer lived in tents and roamed as strangers in the land. They desired a time when they could put down roots and build foundations, and live as owners of the inheritance, having come fully into their destiny.

Faith is required for the journey from promise to inheritance. Do you have promises from God? Do you currently reside in tents, wandering the land until you reach the destination? Are you in between the promise and the land? Faith is required. Don't look at the tent or the desert. When you feel like a wayfarer, don't lose heart. Wait with confident expectation, and trust God to build your home with a firm foundation. He is the great Builder!

1. What have you left behind to follow God? Are you on a journey to an unknown destination?

2. What does waiting with expectation and confidence in God look like on your journey? How have you exercised faith in the in-between places?

3. Who do you know whose faith inspires you to deeper levels with God?

117

Passionate Patience

Romans 5:3-5 (The Message)

There's more to come: We continue to shout our praise even when we're hemmed in with troubles, because we know how troubles can develop passionate patience in us, and how that patience in turn forges the tempered steel of virtue, keeping us alert for whatever God will do next. In alert expectancy such as this, we're never left feeling shortchanged. Quite the contrary—we can't round up enough containers to hold everything God generously pours into our lives through the Holy Spirit!

I can relate to Paul's description of "how troubles can develop passionate patience in us." I love the term "passionate patience." It is not a patience of deadness or passivity. There is not a quality of being stuck, but rather of passion and expectancy embedded with endurance and waiting on the Lord. This patience helps keep us "alert for whatever God will do next." I see in my own life that when I am pressed on all sides with trouble, I hone my focus. The intensity and endurance required during these seasons compel me to set my face on God without compromise or flinching. I believe this is what Paul describes as "alert expectancy."

This "alert expectancy," the constant scanning of the horizon for God, is what leaves us never "feeling shortchanged;" because we can't miss what

God is doing, we are focused and without compromise. We expect to see Him, and we do. Of course, I love the last visual image. Paul says that, in the end, "We can't round up enough containers to hold everything God generously pours into our lives through the Holy Spirit!" I don't know about you, but I could probably round up a lot of containers, but not enough to limit God, who always works in abundance!

1. In what ways do your troubles work to increase your focus on God? Do you know what it is to watch with "alert expectancy?"

2. In what ways have you experienced God's abundance? What has the Holy Spirit poured into your life?

118

Grow Like Grain

Zechariah 9:16-17 (Contemporary English Version)

The LORD God will save them on that day, because they are his people, and they will shine on his land like jewels in a crown. How lovely they will be. Young people will grow there like grain in a field or grapes in a vineyard.

The saving arm of God is coming to you. He is your source of rescue and restoration. We pray with longing for the day when hope and healing have returned, and when we all shine like jewels in God's crown! That shining day—the day of glory and restoration and saving, when we will celebrate the rightness of God and the completeness of His plan for good—how lovely it will be!

Our young people, our sons and daughters, will grow there. They will grow, live, and flourish. They will be like grain in a field, golden and swaying in the breeze, with arms stretched upward in worship to God as they reflect His light and glory. They will grow as grapes in a vineyard, the fruitfulness of God, dripping with goodness and abundance. On that day, we will be saved and restored!

1. *God, we wait with eager anticipation for the day of your salvation and restoration! I pray that you will strengthen the readers' hearts as they long for and wait for the day of completeness for their household and their children.*

2. Can you imagine your son or daughter flourishing like "grain in a field or grapes in a vineyard?" What will that look like in your household?

119

Power To Grasp

Ephesians 3:18-19 (New International Version)

May (you) have power, together with all the Lord's holy people, to grasp how wide and long and high and deep is the love of Christ, and to know this love that surpasses knowledge—that you may be filled to the measure of all the fullness of God.

I have had the privilege at times to listen to people's hearts. I have heard the cries of parents for their children. I have seen their wrestling and struggle. At times, it becomes a wrestling about belief, faith, and the character of God. I have even heard wonderful mothers and fathers doubt that God loves them, and fear the certainty of their own place in God's heart and Kingdom.

I pray for you, reader, during your seasons of wrestling with God and the struggles of life. My deep desire is that you may have the power to understand, as all God's people should, the infinite dimensions of God's love for you. Not you in the abstract, not you on your best day, and not you with conditions and caveats, but all that you are and will be. May you know God's abiding and personal love for you through experience, not through philosophy. You are the beloved, the desired, and the pursued of God. It is you. It has always been you. God cannot love you any more or any less than

He already does. His love for you is complete and full, lacking nothing. No circumstance changes the truth of God's deep abiding desire for you. Once you have experiential knowledge of God's love for YOU, "you will be made complete." You will be filled with fullness of life and power, and all of it comes from God.

1. Do you understand the love of God through experience or philosophy? How would experiential knowledge change you?

2. Do you look to your circumstances to gauge whether you are loved by God? In what way did Jesus's earthly life highlight the seeming contrast between what life looks like and how much God loves us?

3. How did people in scripture know they were loved by God? How did it change their lives?

120

Commission

Deuteronomy 3:28 (New International Version)

But commission Joshua, and encourage and strengthen him, for he will lead this people across and will cause them to inherit the land you will see.

What is your mission? What has God called you to do in your sphere of influence? Here we see Moses being instructed to commission Joshua, and to encourage and strengthen him. Commission means that Moses granted Joshua God's authority and power to carry out his leadership task, and what did God say Joshua would need to fulfill that commission? Courage and strength!

To me, the word "encourage" can seem wimpy. It seems like a "nice" word, but not one that empowers. It's like something you would do for someone when nothing else of any substance can be done. However, when I really look at the word, I see the word COURAGE. En-courage means to fill someone with courage. We all need courage to fulfill our commission from Christ, whatever that may entail. As parents of children with extraordinary needs, we may need a particularly strong dose of courage. Our children too may not feel accepted by the world and may hunger for encouragement, confidence, and strength of heart! They need to feel recognized and affirmed, courageous and confident. They in turn can also be great sources of encouragement for others!

My mission: I am called to inspire courage in those around me. No one should leave a discussion with me with any sense of shame, defeat, or despair. Everyone I come in contact with should be encouraged by me. Each one should be filled with hope and confidence in what God is doing and understand their special part in His work!

1. Think of an interaction with your child that became a difficult one. In what way could you fill your child with courage in that interaction?

2. Consider the people who work with your child on a daily or weekly basis. How can your presence in their environment be a catalyst for courage, inspiration, and strength?

3. Having a child with complex needs can feel isolating. How can you seek out people who fill you with courage and strength?

121

No Matter Where

Isaiah 57:18-19 (Contemporary English Version)

I will heal you, lead you, and give you comfort, until those who are mourning start singing my praises. No matter where you are, I, the LORD, will heal you and give you peace.

Where are you right now? What season are you in? Know that "no matter where you are," God will find you, lead you, and restore you. He will be the one who comforts you and brings healing to your heart and soul. God will bring singing and joy into seasons of mourning. No matter where you are, God will bring you wholeness and peace. No matter where you are.

Give praise to the God who finds you where you are. Sing to the God who changes your mourning into praise. In His Presence, you will be made whole and overflowing with His peace. He will lead, no matter where you are.

1. Where are you? In what ways has God met you in that place?

2. Put your name and that of your child in this verse, post it somewhere in your home, and speak this scripture over your lives. God will heal (name), God will lead (name), and God will give (name) comfort until mourning is turned to praise. No matter where (name) is, God will heal (him/her) and give (him/her) peace.

122

Never Before

Joshua 10:12-14 (Contemporary English Version)

The LORD was helping the Israelites defeat the Amorites that day. So about noon, Joshua prayed to the LORD loud enough for the Israelites to hear: "Our LORD, make the sun stop in the sky over Gibeon, and the moon stand still over Aijalon Valley." So the sun and the moon stopped and stood still until Israel defeated its enemies…The sun stood still and didn't go down for about a whole day. Never before and never since has the LORD done anything like that for someone who prayed. The LORD was really fighting for Israel.

In this passage, Joshua is fighting the enemy. The battle has been lengthy, and the day is wasting away. The sunlight is near gone, and Joshua knows he can't defeat the enemy unless he can see with clarity what would otherwise be hidden and murky. He calls out to God who is helping them. He asks God to stop the sun and the moon, to halt time itself so the sun stays high in the sky and clarity remains for the battle, and that is exactly what happened. The sun stayed high in the sky for "about a whole day!"

We praise God who really fights for us. We praise God who listens to our needs. We raise a joyful shout to the God who intervenes and illuminates the battle until the enemy is defeated. When we are walking with God, we are a people who can shout, "Never before!" God has just done something He has never done before! The sun is bright, the battle continues, and the exposed enemy is defeated!

1. *We thank you, God, for being a God of supernatural interventions when we battle to defeat the enemy and all his plans (e.g., sickness, shame, fear, depression). We invite you in, God. May all the enemy's battle plans be exposed with no place to hide!*

2. What is the enemy your household is fighting? Pray for supernatural illumination today, so the enemy is exposed and defeated.

123

Mission Statement

Luke 4:18-19 (New International Version)

"The Spirit of the Lord is on me, because he has anointed me to proclaim good news to the poor. He has sent me to proclaim freedom for the prisoners and recovery of sight for the blind, to set the oppressed free, to proclaim the year of the Lord's favor."

In Luke, Jesus reads this scripture from the Old Testament (see Isaiah 61:1-2) in the synagogue. He declares that this is His mission statement. He says that the words of Isaiah are fulfilled in Him. He has come to proclaim good news to those who have no good news. He has come to offer people freedom from anything that binds or traps them. He has come to open the eyes of the blind and to proclaim the season of God's favor and grace. This is why Jesus came. This is His mission statement.

What is your mission statement? Why are you here? God asks us to partner with Him in His good work today. He remains forever a God of freedom, healing, and good news. Look around you. Look into the eyes of your children or your spouse. Look around at church and in your community. Look around your nation and around your world. What is your mission?

Every individual is not called to go after and fix every problem. But, we are not individuals. We are a body of believers with Christ at the head. Has He called you to bring good news to your children's educators? Has He called you to pray for breakthrough in the area of cancer or autism? Has He called you to speak freedom to people who have been abused and live in bondage to shame? It is important to know your mission in Him. It is your destiny in Christ. You are meant to bless the world around you.

1. Pray about your identity and destiny in Christ. Allow Him to help you develop a mission statement. Write it in your journal.

2. Pray for revelation of destiny over your children. They are here to change the world. They are meant to be a blessing.

124

Propelled Into Goodness

Jeremiah 29:11 (New International Version)

"For I know the plans I have for you," declares the LORD, "plans to prosper you and not to harm you, plans to give you hope and a future."

When I ask people what helps them get through a difficult time, they sometimes say something to the effect that "knowing that other people have it worse off than me helps me get through." I can understand that approach in the sense that putting our circumstances in perspective and seeing the big picture can be grounding. However, I question whether it is the most life-giving approach. It is essentially choosing to focus on the negative things around us, the unfixed and broken things in our world, rather than focusing on our own individual struggle. But the focus is still on the darkness. Might it not be more in the truth and more life giving to fix our eyes on the glorious future that God speaks over our lives.

I believe that God declares His plans over each of our lives. I believe He calls us forward into an identity, a destiny, and a future that is filled with restoration, healing, and grace. I believe that every season we pass through is ultimately destined for grace in Him. There is no season designed for loss. I believe that, ultimately, it is not fixing the past or the present that helps us, although, that can be a piece of what happens. I believe we are able to move forward even during difficult seasons because we are propelled into God's goodness—the future He declares for us. We are moving toward something in Christ, not stuck in the past or the present. We are being pulled into a beautiful plan where we prosper and know true hope. That is what "gets us through."

1. How are you approaching your present season? Are you able to ask God about the future, or do you feel stuck in the negative of the past or present?

2. How can you focus on God's promises for the future of you and your child? Can you feel these promises propel you forward?

125

Glory to Glory

2 Corinthians 3:18 (The Message)

And so we are transfigured much like the Messiah, our lives gradually becoming brighter and more beautiful as God enters our lives and we become like him.

It is not uncommon to hear people say, "Yeah, it's bad, and it is only going to get worse." Or they say, "I am doing as well as possible under the circumstances. But it's all downhill from here." I have heard talk like this in the line at the grocery store, waiting at the mechanics, and even at church as we pile out after a great sermon and chitchat about recent events in politics, health, weather, or finances. We say this to make conversation, but it represents a worldview that is not from God. God designed us to reflect Him in all His truth, life, and glory.

It is the design of the Father that we are moving from glory to glory, "becoming brighter and more beautiful as God enters our lives and we become like him." Meditate on this truth. As a son of the Father, a daughter of the most High God, you are designed to become brighter and brighter. You are designed to keep moving forward, to rise up as you come to reflect God more and more. You are not designed to be stuck, to decay, or decline. Your life is designed to have forward momentum, always moving from glory to glory. Whatever your feelings, and whatever people are chatting about, the truth is broader, deeper, and more wonderful than you can ever imagine.

1. Have you ever made casual conversation about how things are going from bad to worse? Is this consistent with God's plan as revealed to us in the scriptures?

2. In what ways are you moving from glory to glory? If you feel stuck, how can you agree with the scripture and embrace your destiny to move from glory to glory?

126

Encircling Peace

Zechariah 9:8, 10 (Contemporary English Version)

God says, "I will stand guard to protect my temple from those who come to attack. I know what's happening, and no one will mistreat my people ever again.... I, the LORD, will take away war chariots and horses from Israel and Jerusalem. Bows that were made for battle will be broken. I will bring peace to nations, and your king will rule from sea to sea. His kingdom will reach from the Euphrates River across the earth."

God is speaking. What is He saying? He is talking about standing guard over you and protecting His temple from enemies who would attack it. He is encamped around your household in protection. He says, "I know what's happening, and no one will mistreat my people ever again." He sees the enemy, the attack, and the injustice. He speaks peace over you and your children: peace near and peace far, encircling you. The weapons you have formed for your protection will be broken and taken away because peace is coming to reign in your household and to rain down upon it, too.

Let us pray from a secure place of peace because we know that God wins the victory for us in every circumstance. He gives us peace and rest from our enemies. Our King has come to rule from sea to sea. His Kingdom of peace, life, and provision reaches across the earth.

1. How have you and your children known God as your protector and defender?

2. What will God's peace and Kingdom life look like in your household?

127

Between

Romans 4:17 (New International Version)

As it is written: "I have made you {Abraham} a father of many nations." He is our father in the sight of God, in whom he believed—the God who gives life to the dead and calls into being things that were not.

We have a God who calls into being things that are not. He speaks and brings forth those things that do not yet exist. He is a God of the future, speaking into destiny as He calls forth things that will be, but are not yet. When He speaks, life happens, dead things are raised, empty places filled, and broken places healed. He spoke to Abraham about a son and generations to come. Abraham heard the word, he understood the promise, and he entered into covenant with a God who called him by name and told him who he was.

But there is tension in that "between" place. The tension is present during the waiting season that occurs between God's word and promises fulfilled. Abraham waited twenty-five years from when he heard God's promise to when he held his son Isaac. David waited about ten years from when he was anointed king, to when he sat on the throne. There is a place of longing and grieving when we are living in the "not yet" time, the "in-between" season, the time when our circumstances are not yet what they should be and not what they will be.

Lord, you are the God who gives life to the dead. You call into being things that are not yet. Thank you for your promises, and your spoken words that bring healing, restoration, and purpose. I pray for the reader today as he waits for your promises in his life to be fulfilled. I pray for the reader that longs for her destiny to meet her in the now. I pray for the parents that love their children and long for breakthrough in the now. May you give them strength, courage, and faith for the journey.

1. What promises do you hold on to from God? Journal about promises fulfilled and promises still in the waiting.

2. How can you balance the tension of waiting and longing in the between seasons? Ask God to enlighten your heart today with His word and revelation in this area.

128

TENDER GOD

ISAIAH 57:15 (THE MESSAGE)

A Message from the high and towering God, who lives in Eternity, whose name is Holy: "I live in the high and holy places, but also with the low-spirited, the spirit-crushed, And what I do is put new spirit in them, get them up and on their feet again."

God is towering, almighty, holy, and eternal. God is also near, tender, intimate, and in the moment. He is both big enough and small enough to meet all your needs. He sees you and knows you. He is near to you when your spirit is low and crushed and your heart has been trod upon and left in the dirt. He sees you. He loves you. He puts you on your feet and fills you up with a whole new spirit. There's newness inside you—a lifting up and a filling—all from God to you.

Thank you, God, for being both eternal and near. You are in the moment with us; you see our future and call us into our purpose. You see our hearts and you know when our spirits are crushed. I pray, God, that you will visit each reader today. I pray that they will know their tender God, the God who fills them with a new and living Spirit—the God who brings them to their feet and sets them on their path again. You are a renewing and restoring God.

1. What season are you and your children in now? How is your spirit doing? Can you invite God into your now and ask Him to heal and renew your spirit?

2. How has God been a personal God to you and your household? How have you experienced His restoration in your journey with God?

129

Waiting Saturday

Romans 8:11 (Contemporary English Version)

Yet God raised Jesus to life! God's Spirit now lives in you, and he will raise you to life by his Spirit.

Sometimes, I meditate about the sequence of events during the crucifixion and resurrection. Christ died on Friday and was raised from the dead on the third day, Sunday, but what about Saturday? Scripture is conspicuously silent about that in-between day. In some ways, Saturday may be the day I appreciate the most, through experience and personal history. Saturday was the day after the glory departed. It may have been the longest day ever. The Saturday of the Easter season contains within it the heaviness of waiting in the midst of loss while searching for faith for more than is seen. Saturday is where many of us live much of our lives—feeling the loss of yesterday but not yet seeing the resurrection and restoration of Easter Sunday.

Father, we choose to wait with expectant faith through the seasons between loss and resurrection. We commit ourselves to faith, belief, hope, and joy during the waiting seasons of life, the seasons when restoration seems next to impossible. We believe that the resurrection spirit of God abides in us, and therefore, we know victory draws near!

1. At this time of your life, can you most relate to Good Friday, Waiting Saturday, or Easter Sunday?

2. What difference does it make to you to know that God's resurrection Spirit lives inside you?

130

Yet I Will

Habakkuk 3:17-18 (Amplified Bible)

Though the fig tree does not blossom and there is no fruit on the vines, {though} the product of the olive fails and the fields yield no food, though the flock is cut off from the fold and there are no cattle in the stalls, Yet I will rejoice in the Lord; I will exult in the {victorious} God of my salvation!

There are seasons in which we find ourselves weary from having prayed so long for breakthrough, but without seeing the fruit of our labor. This is an important choice point. It becomes a matter of will to praise the attributes of God: His person, His character, and His promises. Even when we don't see them materialize, we need to praise Him and rejoice in Him. Yet I will rejoice in the Lord! I have decided; It is a matter of my will. Yet will I rejoice! I will exult in the victorious God who saves me! I will rejoice in my victorious God, even when I can't yet see the victory!

We rejoice in you God. You are our victory and our salvation! Even in our weariness, we praise you. Even in our lack, we exult you. We have decided to live our life with this stance before you. Though we see no blossoms and no fruit, and though we lack food and resources, even so, God, we praise you. We rejoice in your Person, your attributes, and your loving kindness toward us and toward our children. During the waiting, throughout seasons of lack, and before the breakthrough, we praise you! We choose to live rejoicing in you, God, always in you.

1. Praising God during seasons of lack is a matter of choice. It is a decision about what is most important and Who is most important. How can we teach our children to rejoice in and through every season of life?

2. What attributes of God are you praising today? Make a list of His qualities and attributes that bring your heart to a place of rejoicing! Praise Him even though things are unfixed and unfinished in your life.

131

Thoughts

Psalm 139:17-18 (Amplified Bible)

How precious and weighty also are Your thoughts to me, O God! How vast is the sum of them! If I could count them, they would be more in number than the sand. When I awoke, {could I count to the end} I would still be with You.

We have a personal God who is intimately involved with His people. He has created us, entered into covenant promises with us, redeemed us, and directed us. He is not far away, nor is He amorphous and unformed. He is not without direction or purpose. Rather, His thoughts are toward you, your household, your community, and your world. His thoughts are purposeful, with design and direction for good, restoration, and wholeness. His thoughts and plans are so numerous and developed that He has no lack of purpose; He is not stuck or dumbfounded. He is not surprised or without solution. He has the answer to every problem, freedom from every bondage, and healing for every infirmity.

1. God has thoughts and plans, direction and focus. Ask Him to share His thoughts with you today. What is He thinking about and planning?

2. Ask God how you can partner with Him to bring about freedom, goodness, and wholeness to the world around you.

132

GIVE

LUKE 6:38
(NEW INTERNATIONAL VERSION)

Give, and it will be given to you. A good measure, pressed down, shaken together and running over, will be poured into your lap. For with the measure you use, it will be measured to you.

During times of hardship, it is easy to feel that your resources are stretched to the limit. You may feel lack in your life in many areas (e.g., time, money, forgiveness, rest). This feeling of lack can be intensified for parents who are caring for a child with illness or other specific needs. The scripture from Luke is a wonderful visual picture of the abundance of God. I am often tempted to feel lack, rather than abundance, in my circumstances. I may feel like curling up and hoarding everything I have, trying not to lose anything else.

I have learned to focus on God's abundance, rather than my lack. I have also learned to trust His abundance. At times, this requires a specific and determined decision of the will. It requires me to live in the opposite spirit—opposite to my feelings of lack or poverty. It is generally when I start to curl up and hang onto things too tightly that I realize my heart needs to trust God. I need to cultivate a living faith in His provision, His good heart, and His abundant resources. I must decide to give in good measure, and believe that it will be returned to me in good measure, pressed down, shaken together and running over, poured into my lap!

1. Have you ever been tempted to live by clinging to what you are afraid to lose? What are signals to you in your life that this is happening?

2. In what ways have you tried to cultivate an opposite spirit? How has giving something away left you more filled up?

133

Trustworthy

Hebrews 11:11-12 (Amplified Bible)

Because of faith also Sarah herself received physical power to conceive a child, even when she was long past the age for it, because she considered {God} Who had given her the promise to be reliable and trustworthy and true to His word. So from one man, though he was physically as good as dead, there have sprung descendants whose number is as the stars of heaven and as countless as the innumerable sands on the seashore.

This scripture gets right to the point. It paints a vivid picture of Sarah, who needed physical power, and Abraham, who was "as good as dead." They had a promise from God. Would the promise be enough to sustain their faith for the twenty-five years it took to receive the child? Hebrews says that Sarah considered God to be reliable and trustworthy, true to His Word. That is the substance of faith isn't it? Do we consider God to be true to His Word, trustworthy, and reliable? Can we hold onto a promise over years without any visible change in our circumstances?

God is reliable. God is trustworthy. God is true to His Word. God is faithful. God is good. God is with you. I pray for your heart in the waiting times between promise and fruition. I pray that you will have a living faith that sustains and guides you. May your vision be on the prize and on the One who brings all things together. Each word of His promises resonates through eternity. His words do not become void or falter.

1. Are there promises that you have held onto over years without visible signs of breakthrough?

2. When your faith falters, do you have family or friends who rally to encourage you and pray over you? Remember, God is reliable and trustworthy. His Word is true and will come to completion.

134

High Places

Habakkuk 3:19 (Amplified Bible)

The Lord God is my Strength, my personal bravery, and my invincible army; He makes my feet like hinds' feet and will make me to walk {not to stand still in terror, but to walk} and make {spiritual} progress upon my high places {of trouble, suffering, or responsibility}!

This is a scripture with many visual images and layers of meaning. First, it declares, "The Lord God is my Strength…" He is my strength, and He is my personal bravery. He is my army. He is invincible. He fights for me against my enemies. This is a personal truth about a personal God, an enduring truth about an enduring God, and an invincible truth about an invincible God. He is mine, and He strengthens me.

God makes my feet like "hinds' feet," like a deer walking up a high mountain. In scripture, a mountain can be used to depict an intense spiritual place. This may be a place of spiritual ecstasy and intimacy, as with the Moses and the glory of God on the mountain. In contrast, the mountain may be a place requiring extreme endurance and courage. You may feel the lack of oxygen up in the heights and the difficulty of climbing and navigating the terrain. But the Lord makes you to walk, "not to stand still in terror, but to walk" without falling or becoming stuck. He causes you to make "spiritual progress" in the high places "of trouble, suffering, or responsibility." Within the intense places of squeezing and pressure, the places of struggling and wrestling, God leads you to make progress and to have sure footing.

1. In what ways are the spiritual truths of this passage personal to you?

2. How have you experienced mountains in your life? In what ways has God given you sure footing during intense and high places or seasons?

135

Perfect in Love

1 John 4:18 (Amplified Bible)

There is no fear in love {dread does not exist}, but full-grown (complete, perfect) love turns fear out of doors and expels every trace of terror! For fear brings with it the thought of punishment, and {so} he who is afraid has not reached the full maturity of love {is not yet grown into love's complete perfection}.

Fear is such a draining emotion. It can find you thinking about the past and the present, and give you false predictions about the future. There is a power to fear that chases you, finds you, and haunts you. You can do several things to rid yourself of the spirit of fear. You can think positive thoughts, focus on the scripture, and spend time with Jesus. The most powerful antidote for fear, however, is love—perfect love. When we become totally immersed in God's great, mighty, and perfect love for us and our children, fear is cast out. There is no torment, but rather we are made perfect in love, lacking nothing but fear.

When I am fearful, I realize that I am not living with an awareness of the deep, eternal, echoing, and fully present love of God. If I was aware of God's true love for me and my child in any small measure, I would be immersed in thinking about Him and His glory, His perfection. Fear would be cast off, and I would be made complete, just as God is complete.

1. The way to be made perfect, lacking nothing, is to be immersed in love and to cast out fear. Have you been made perfect in love? I encourage you to invite God into your life in a way that shows you His complete and powerful love for you and your children.

2. Have you tried to make yourself perfect in ways other than immersing yourself in God's love? Have you attempted to cast off fear in other ways? How successful has this been?

136

Risk

Hebrews 11:6 (The Message)

It's impossible to please God apart from faith. And why? Because anyone who wants to approach God must believe both that he exists and that he cares enough to respond to those who seek him.

My personality is fairly conservative. I might be described as responsible and steady. I am not generally a risk-taker at heart. I do not need a lot of new things going on to be happy; I actually prefer the simple things. This aspect of God's character stretches me. Faith stretches me because it involves risk, a reliance on things not seen, and a joyful expectancy when realism does not demonstrate anything good. It is impossible to please God apart from faith in things that cannot be touched or seen, and that may not seem real enough to be relied on. Faith can feel risky.

A belief that God exists is not enough to approach Him wholeheartedly. There must be the faith, sometimes against all that assaults our senses, that God cares enough to respond to those who seek Him. Faith that God exists AND that He will respond. We must bank everything on those two things in order to please God. We must live with the joyful expectancy that what is unseen will break through in love to respond when we seek Him.

1. Does faith feel risky or responsible? Has your journey with God ever brought you to a place where faith in the unseen felt like a leap in the dark?

2. In what ways has your journey with your child tested your faith? How has your faith been enriched?

137

Sing and Shout

Zephaniah 3:14-15 (Amplified Bible)

Sing, O Daughter of Zion; shout, O Israel! Rejoice, be in high spirits and glory with all your heart, O Daughter of Jerusalem {in that day}. {For then it will be that} the Lord has taken away the judgments against you; He has cast out your enemy. The King of Israel, even the Lord {Himself}, is in the midst of you; {and after He has come to you} you shall not experience or fear evil any more.

Parents face many obstacles in their journey with their kids. No matter who you are or where you live, there are challenges to parenting well. Parents who are raising children with specific needs face challenges above the norm. One of these challenges is the monumental amount of advice, debate, and judgment you can receive from those around you about how to "fix" certain difficulties in your home and in the lives of your children. "If only you would do this!" or "There is no way I would ever do that." Depending on the topic, the amount of debate can become intense and condemning. What is the "right thing" to do? What is the "right path" to take? Judgments against you can come from the right and the left, sometimes from places you least anticipate.

These verses in Zephaniah are encouraging. They invite each of us to rejoice and celebrate wholeheartedly. "The Lord has taken away the judgments against you; He has cast out your enemy." God is with you. He comes to be near you, to cover you, and to fill you up. There is no condemnation from Him. The judgment you may feel from the people around you is not what God feels toward you. He embraces you and warms you. The King is with you, now and forever. He loves the heart you have toward your child, and your aspiration to do the right thing. "The King of Israel, even the Lord [Himself], is in the midst of you; [and after He has come to you] you shall not experience or fear evil any more." What happens when God is with you? You shall not experience or fear evil any more.

1. Have you felt judged, blamed, or condemned as you try to parent your child well? Does the judgment come from others, yourself, or both? Let it go today.

2. Invite the King to be with you. He comes without condemnation. There is no rejection in Him. You will fear disaster no more. You will know complete freedom.

138

If You Are

Luke 23:39
(The Message)

One of the criminals hanging alongside cursed him: "Some Messiah you are! Save yourself! Save us!"

When I think of the cross, I remember Mary grieving, John at the foot of the cross, and Peter denying Jesus. I think about who wasn't there, the scattering of the disciples. And I think of the thief who said, "If you are the Christ, save yourself and us." This was as if to say, "Fix your situation to show me that God is really with you. If God were really with you, your situation would look better." What a subtle invitation to believe a lie. "If God is really with you, prove it." It reminds me of the temptation of Jesus in the desert, when the Adversary came and said, "If you are the son of God, command these stones to become bread" (Matthew 4:3; NIV). He challenged Jesus to fix His situation in order to demonstrate that He is God's Son.

It is certainly not bad to try to problem-solve and fix situations. However, the lie is in the implication that your situation must be resolved in order to demonstrate that you are God's beloved son or daughter. The lie is the suggestion that your circumstance speaks to whether you are loved by the God of the universe. We cannot look to our circumstances to make conclusions about God. We must start with what we know about God, and then make conclusions about our circumstances. God is good all the time. God is faithful all the time. God brings good out of every situation. God loves you and desires you all the time.

1. What do you believe about God? If you are uncertain, start here. Ask God to reveal His basic and unchanging nature to you. Then start with what you know about God to decide what you know about your circumstances.

2. Have you been invited to believe the lie that your circumstances somehow demonstrate God's feelings toward you? Do you see the lie? How can you change your belief system to focus on the truth of God's desire and love for you?

139

God is Good

Psalm 118:1 (Amplified Bible)

Give thanks to the Lord, for He is good; for His mercy and loving-kindness endure forever!

We each need foundational beliefs, things that are at the core of how we live. The foundations are the things that don't change, even when all other things do. About these things, we say, "I may not know much, but I do know this..." What are your foundational beliefs about God?

One of my foundational spiritual beliefs is that God is good, all the time, forever and ever, and in every way throughout eternity. This is a core belief. There are many opportunities in this world to doubt or wrestle with this statement. It is important to figure out what your belief is in this area. If you don't know what is true, your circumstances will try to tell you what to believe.

What is more real: what you see or what you don't see? What is truer: what your circumstances tell you or what God says? It is important to know what you believe in this area before trouble comes. You will need to rely on your foundations when trouble is shaking your house.

God is good all the time. I know it; I believe it! It is a truth beyond the limitations of my circumstance—an eternal, basic truth. The character of God never changes because He is good forever. I pray for you right now, reader, that you will be covered with His truth today. I pray that the glory of His goodness will break into your circumstances, and you will know that He is good to you, to your child, and to your household, right now and always. Be immersed in this truth today, and let this foundation change your perspective on everything else.

1. What are your core beliefs about God? How have they impacted your life choices?

2. If you truly understood the vast, unrelenting goodness of God, how would your life change? Would you see your circumstances differently? Would your emotions change?

140

Be Strong

Deuteronomy 31:6 (Amplified Bible)

Be strong, courageous, and firm; fear not, nor be in terror before them, for it is the Lord your God Who goes with you; He will not fail you or forsake you.

It takes courage to face the Adversary, to combat the Enemy and remove obstacles. It takes courage to stand firm. But be assured, you are the beloved of God. It is impossible for Him to abandon you. It would go against His very nature and being. Know that whatever enemy you and your family face today, God goes with you. Indeed, that is the very reason that we need not fear. If we look at the size of the obstacle or the tentacles of the Enemy, we may tremble with fear. But if we gaze on the One who is with us, we are filled with courage. God will not fail you! He will not forsake you, abandon you, or leave you in the lurch. So be strong and courageous, friend, and stand firm in His promises and Presence.

1. What is your life verse? How does it inspire you to attain victory in Christ?

2. In what ways can you inspire your children to be filled with God's courage?

141

Into the Sea

Mark 11:22-24 (Amplified Bible)

And Jesus, replying, said to them, Have faith in God {constantly}. Truly I tell you, whoever says to this mountain, Be lifted up and thrown into the sea! and does not doubt at all in his heart but believes that what he says will take place, it will be done for him. For this reason I am telling you, whatever you ask for in prayer, believe (trust and be confident) that it is granted to you, and you will {get it}.

Here, Jesus urges His followers to have faith in God constantly. He wants us to have an abiding and enduring faith that is rooted and grounded in our whole journey with God. What amazing words from Jesus—that mountains will be thrown into the sea at our command. We must live without doubt in our hearts, believing that our words can and will make things happen, change, and become rooted or uprooted. We must ask in prayer with belief, trust, and confidence that we will receive answers from God in His time. Sometimes it feels hard to make sense of these words. I pray that Jesus will reveal to you what He is urging you to believe. I pray that He will tell you about the life you are designed to live and embrace.

One thing seems certain. Jesus wants us not only to pray for what we need, but also to live with a posture of faith and belief. After the actual prayers are said, the posture in which we live is important. The spirit that we carry is important to God. Do we say a prayer and then live in worry? Do we brood and ruminate about all the possibilities, concerned about the outcome and timing of everything? Jesus says NO! We are to pray and then live expectantly, confidently, and in belief, faith, and trust. We can expect mountains to be removed and thrown into the sea!

1. I pray that Jesus reveals more and more to your heart as you pray through this passage and make it your own. Pray through this scripture throughout the week and journal about what God reveals to you.

2. In what ways are you tempted to live in a posture of doubt or concern? What encourages you to live with faith and expectation in God's power and goodness?

142

FOCUS ON JESUS

MATTHEW 14:29-31 (THE MESSAGE)

Jumping out of the boat, Peter walked on the water to Jesus. But when he looked down at the waves churning beneath his feet, he lost his nerve and started to sink. He cried, "Master, save me!" Jesus didn't hesitate. He reached down and grabbed his hand. Then he said, "Faint-heart, what got into you?"

I love to read and meditate on the exchanges between Jesus and the people throughout the scripture. They are so precious and revealing to me. I love Peter and Jesus in this exchange. Can't you just imagine it? The terror of the storm and seeing a 'ghost' followed by a sudden boldness as Jesus literally walks closer to the boat. I love the boldness that rose up in Peter's heart when he recognized Jesus in the midst of the storm. How revealing it is about their relationship and Peter's own journey with God. But let's face it, there were a lot of waves. When Peter saw the waves churning at his feet, he lost heart and began to sink. I know both the feeling of boldness and faint-heartedness, that sinking feeling.

Let us pray together today as you read this. We declare to the heavens that we want our children back! I pray over your household and your child, reader. I pray for all those in our churches and communities who see their children trapped and struggling today. We want our children back! Let us focus on Jesus's face. Let us shout together in boldness, joining in the amazing adventure with God, believing and doing the impossible. May you join Jesus in the impossible today!

1. Has your journey with God ever involved moments of terror—churning waves, seeing ghosts, and needing the impossible to become possible?

2. Do you feel bold or faint-hearted today? Focus on the face of Jesus, and believe the impossible.

143

Ask Boldly

James 1:5-8 (The Message)

If you don't know what you're doing, pray to the Father. He loves to help. You'll get his help, and won't be condescended to when you ask for it. Ask boldly, believingly, without a second thought. People who "worry their prayers" are like wind-whipped waves. Don't think you're going to get anything from the Master that way, adrift at sea, keeping all your options open.

These verses speak to me personally so much. One of my journeys as a praying child of God has been to grow from a person who "worries" my prayers, to one who comes boldly before Father God to ask for what I need. I remember at one point hearing myself say things like "Oh my goodness, things are going so badly for them. We all really need to pray together for that situation." I realized that what I was really saying was "Let's all worry together for them." Yes, I know I used the word "pray" but I really meant, "worry pray"—shooting up prayers of anxiety and wringing my hands. Indeed, I felt adrift at sea.

If there is one thing I have realized, it is that the scripture tells us that the way we approach prayer is important. I call it my "posture" as I am praying, worshiping, and soaking in God's presence. It is important to have a posture of expectation, trust, and confidence as we approach God and lift our intercessions to the throne. There is spiritual release and power as we ask "boldly, believingly, without a second thought." When we ask with second thoughts, we are like those who "worry their prayers." We are adrift.

1. What is your posture like as you interact with God and approach His throne? What is your level of expectation, trust, and confidence?

2. Have you ever worried and called it prayer? Can you relate to the description in James of feeling like "wind-shipped waves" and "adrift at sea?"

3. How can you adjust your posture before God as you intercede for your children and your household?

144

Open Eyes

2 Kings 6:15-17 (Amplified Bible)

When the servant of the man of God rose early and went out, behold, an army with horses and chariots was around the city. Elisha's servant said to him, Alas, my master! What shall we do? {Elisha} answered, Fear not; for those with us are more than those with them. Then Elisha prayed, Lord, I pray You, open his eyes that he may see. And the Lord opened the young man's eyes, and he saw, and behold, the mountain was full of horses and chariots of fire round about Elisha.

Many things are important. It is important to know that what we don't see is more real and definitive than what we see. It is important that we "Fear not!" no matter what we think we know or think we see. Believing in the unseen and trusting without fear releases power and goodness into our lives. It keeps us from being stuck, small, and constrained. Elisha knew this, so he prayed for his servant. "Open his eyes that he may see." Then the servant saw and understood that they were surrounded by an army of angels. Indeed, those who were with Elisha and his servant were greater than the enemy armies.

Let's pray together reader. I pray that God will open your eyes and allow you to see, and that in seeing you will believe. I pray that your whole framework of thinking will be changed by what you see. May you live with the deep understanding that what is invisible is real, amazing, and glorious, while what is visible is fleeting and incomplete. Fear not reader! God surrounds you and your children with His angels and His glorious presence.

1. Do you believe in the unseen? How have you experienced the invisible?

2. In what ways have your experiences changed the way you live?

145

Decide

Psalm 27: 1-3 (Contemporary English Version)

You, LORD, are the light that keeps me safe. I am not afraid of anyone. You protect me, and I have no fears. Brutal people may attack and try to kill me, but they will stumble. Fierce enemies may attack, but they will fall. Armies may surround me, but I won't be afraid; war may break out, but I will trust you.

Getting through life with a sense of grounding and peace rarely has to do with the absence of conflict. The centering that we have must come from our trust in the God who is with us. Here, the psalmist talks about not living in fear when enemies surround and attack. Why? Because "I will trust" in the Lord!

Sometimes that last part, saying, "I will trust you," requires a determined decision. When you find yourself surrounded by enemies (e.g., illness, financial difficulties, rejection, depression), and you begin to fear, you must decide whether to trust God. Will you focus your heart and mind on the Light that keeps you safe? There are seasons of life when we must decide and re-decide several times a day.

I pray for you and your household today. As you read these very words, I pray that you will be strengthened inside to choose trust in the Light that keeps you safe. Do not be deceived by the sight of the enemy. Be focused, centered, and planted in the Lord who saves you.

1. In what ways can you focus on the Light today?

2. I encourage you to watch your thoughts throughout the day. When you notice fear, decide to enter into trust.

146

Counselor

Psalm 16: 7 (New International Version)

I will praise the LORD, who counsels me; even at night my heart instructs me.

If there is one thing that parents need, it is wisdom! If you are a parent of a child with special medical, learning, behavioral, or emotional needs, you may find yourself at a particular loss for how to approach a challenge or overcome an obstacle. We praise our God that He is filled with wisdom, knowledge, and understanding. Because He is a relational God, He imparts His wisdom to us through His Spirit. Here, the psalmist praises God for providing him with counsel and understanding.

Let's meditate on the second part of the verse. This can be interpreted in two ways. One implication is that God's Spirit instructs our hearts even when we are sleeping. Even as we rest, God is imparting His knowledge and wisdom to us for our situation. Have you ever wrestled with a difficulty before deciding to "sleep on it," only to waken with a better understanding? God can instruct you even as you slumber. Secondly, the instruction of the Spirit comes even in the night seasons, those dark seasons of the soul when we cry out to God for help and rescue. During the night seasons, God counsels us and imparts wisdom.

1. Do you trust God enough to provide for you while you sleep and rest? Have you ever been aware of God's presence during the night, perhaps in a dream or an idea received in sleep?

2. How have you experienced God's counsel during a dark season?

147

Parental Blessing

Psalm 27:10 (Contemporary English Version)

Even if my father and mother should desert me, you will take care of me.

We are born into families on this earth. Some of our growing up experiences were life giving and some of them were challenging and difficult. Not everyone has received the blessing of their parents. Not everyone grew up with parents that saw them through God's eyes, that called out the gold in them, and that loved them unconditionally. There may have been shame and dishonor. You may feel that you were rejected or deserted by the people that should have blessed you and covered you.

We are each called to be a blessing and covering for our children. We are to call forth their gifts, provide them a place of refuge, and fill them with courage for their future. But for every child that does not have parental blessing and refuge, God is there to lift them up. If you are such a child, read Psalm 27 with me right now. God receives you, He lifts you up, and He cares for you! He covers you with parental blessing, He fills you with courage, He gives you identity, and sees your gifts. He calls you into significance. Let's do the same for our children!

1. Have you received blessing and covering from your parents? How have you blessed and received your children?

2. In what ways have you been received and lifted up by God? Do you know God as your Abba Father?

148

Seen and Known

Psalm 139: 1-6 (The Message)

God, investigate my life; get all the facts firsthand. I'm an open book to you; even from a distance, you know what I'm thinking. You know when I leave and when I get back; I'm never out of your sight. You know everything I'm going to say before I start the first sentence. I look behind me and you're there, then up ahead and you're there, too—your reassuring presence, coming and going. This is too much, too wonderful—I can't take it all in!

It is important to understand that God is big, eternal, all-powerful, and ever present, even while He is also intimate, personal, and relational with us. Let's meditate today about God's nearness to us. How intimate, personal, and knowing He is. The God of the universe is with you now as you read these words on this day in this moment. He sees you. He hears you. You are known, loved, and understood. He cares enough to search you out in the deep places. He knows you better than you know yourself. You are His delight and His desire. His longing is for you.

We offer ourselves to you, Lord. We give you our thoughts and our actions. You know when we depart and when we come back in. I am seen by you and loved. You are small enough to be present with me always. You surround me with your presence, behind and ahead, coming and going together. This is too much…too wonderful! I can't take it all in, yet I believe!

1. God is both big enough and small enough to meet you in every place and with every need. How have you known this personal God? Have you felt intimacy and personal impact from the God of the universe?

2. In what ways can you set yourself before God and invite Him in? Do you believe He is good and finds His delight in you? How can you foster this intimate relationship?

149

Move Forward

Numbers 14:1-4 (Contemporary English Version)

After the Israelites heard the report from the twelve men who had explored Canaan, the people cried all night and complained to Moses and Aaron, "We wish we had died in Egypt or somewhere out here in the desert! Is the LORD leading us into Canaan, just to have us killed and our women and children captured? We'd be better off in Egypt." Then they said to one another, "Let's choose our own leader and go back."

Sometimes, God comes and tells us that He is leading us to a new and better place! He is freeing us from bondage and calling us into a new freedom with more life and greater possibilities. What an adventure! Leaving a known place for an unknown, yet promised place. Trusting God, you travel with your children and family through process and journey encountering obstacles and enemies unforeseen. The promise of a new land and a better place may eventually begin to sound far off, like an echo, a thin sound spread out in the distance. Is the promise reliable and true? Is it as reliable and true as the known land of slavery you left?

It is recorded that when Spanish Conquistador Hernando Cortez landed in Mexico in 1519, he burned all of his ships. He knew that while on a journey to enter a new land there would be the temptation to turn back to what is known. He wanted to remove the option of turning back, to increase the focus on what is ahead. Retreat was not an option. In our lives, journey is important. Moving forward is important. Focusing on promise is important. There is no way to bypass this truth, no short cuts, and no blessing from retreat. There are new lands to be conquered and enemies to be defeated (e.g., cancer, autism, learning disabilities, abuse, fear, shame). There is promise and inheritance waiting for you. Move forward!

1. We may feel more brave when journeying alone than when our children are a part of the exodus to an unknown land. How do you teach your children to focus on what is ahead and trust in God's promises?

2. Have you ever been tempted to go back to a known place from the past? How do you keep moving forward with God and cut out the option of retreat?

150

Focus our Thoughts

Philippians 4:8 (New International Version)

Finally, brothers and sisters, whatever is true, whatever is noble, whatever is right, whatever is pure, whatever is lovely, whatever is admirable—if anything is excellent or praiseworthy—think about such things.

There is so much to fill our minds: jokes, concerns, predictions, speculations, judgments, tasks, and determinations. At times, we may feel that we can't keep up with it all. There's so much swirling through our brain, floating through our dreams and sleep, marching through our thoughts during the day. God calls out to us and invites us to focus our thoughts on His Kingdom—the Kingdom of all light, goodness, mercy, and glory. Say it with me: Everything that is true, noble, right, pure, lovely, admirable, excellent, and praiseworthy—think on these things.

Yielding our thoughts to God is so important. We give power to whatever we meditate on. Let us meditate on what is true, and think about noble things, right things. Let's notice what is pure and lovely, and focus on the admirable. Let's meditate on what is excellent and worthy of all praise. Think about these things, drink them in, meditate on them, dream about them, and share them with others. Let them be the declaration of your heart. Focus on the things you want to become increasingly powerful in your life.

1. Consider writing a journal entry about your child today. Write down each one of his or her qualities and character traits (whatever is true and noble), and then describe how each quality is alive in your child's life. You might write about your child's treatment progress this year, the positive impact of the treatment/academic team, or how good friends have lifted your child up.

2. How easy is it for you to lend your thoughts to these things? Have you experienced the power that thoughts and meditations have?

151

Overflowing Life

John 10:10 (Amplified Bible)

The thief comes only in order to steal and kill and destroy. I came that they may have and enjoy life, and have it in abundance (to the full, till it overflows).

Jesus tells us there is a thief. The thief comes to us with a purpose and plan. His agenda is to steal, kill, and destroy. Have you felt his presence, his impact, and his threats? Do you recognize his plan in your life, his words in your ear, and his presence to take away and reduce your power and purpose? Has he stolen things from you, killed, and sought to destroy your household?

Jesus has come to save you and your household from the thief. Jesus has come that you may have life. He has come so that your life, your children's lives, and the lives of all those who believe and abide in Him will be abundant. The life Jesus gives is not merely survival living; it is abundant, full, and overflowing life. Never-ending life is yours. Plentiful life, enough to flow over and bless others, is provided to you and your children through Jesus and His work in your life. The thief will not have his way. You will not be emptied and destroyed. God brings life to fill you up. He brings restoration, healing, and renewal. You will be filled up and overflowing with life.

1. Have you felt the presence of the thief in your life? Have you known the abundant life that Jesus gives?

2. In what ways have you seen restoration and filling in your household? What areas of restoration are you still praying and longing for? I pray that you will know restoration and renewal in all areas of your life. I pray that your children will be restored to full health, peace, and life.

152

Ask and Imagine

Ephesians 3:20-21 (New International Version)

Now to him who is able to do immeasurably more than all we ask or imagine, according to his power that is at work within us, to him be glory in the church and in Christ Jesus throughout all generations, for ever and ever! Amen.

What a wonderful scripture. Hallelujah! Sometimes I can't even believe how wonderful the truth really is. What is the truth? The truth is that God is good all the time. The truth is that His power is at work within us, the same power that raised Jesus from the dead. The truth is that God is able to do "immeasurably more than all we ask or imagine." This is what brings Him glory! I don't know about you, but this scripture encourages me to ask and imagine, and then to expect immeasurably more goodness, more power, and more glory from Him!

What do you ask for? What do you envision, imagine, and dream about? Let's ask together and dream together. Let's do all this, and then live in expectation that we will see His goodness pour out like a river, in abundance, overflowing. Asking is important; having a vision is important; living with the expectation of God's power and goodness is important. Let's do this together, today and always.

1. Think about your child today. Let's ask for what she needs. Let's dream God's dreams for him. I live expectantly with you, looking for God's goodness.

2. In what areas of life have you seen God's power and glory at work? How has He surprised you with abundant goodness?

153

RIVER AND FRUIT

EZEKIEL 47:12 (THE MESSAGE)

But the river itself, on both banks, will grow fruit trees of all kinds. Their leaves won't wither, the fruit won't fail. Every month they'll bear fresh fruit because the river from the Sanctuary flows to them. Their fruit will be for food and their leaves for healing.

In this passage, an angel takes Ezekiel on a journey and shows him the dimensions of the temple as well as things that will usher forth from the temple. In these verses, the angel has described a river that will flow from the temple out into the land/community. The river will become deeper and deeper the farther it flows from the temple. The flowing water from the temple will produce supernatural fruitfulness. Fruit trees of all kinds will grow on both banks. Their leaves will never fall and their fruit will be ready for harvest monthly rather than yearly. The fruit and leaves will provide nourishment and healing.

My prayer as I read this passage has to do with the theme of fruitfulness. I pray that the river that flows from the temple of God will nourish you and provide for you. I pray that you will know the power of your prayers, and that every breakthrough you seek will come to fruition. May you see the coming of your King. I pray that your season of waiting will come to an end and be replaced with a season of fruitfulness in all areas. May you know God's abundant blessings and provision in this season.

1. In what areas have you been praying for a breakthrough? Have you been praying for your children, your marriage, and your finances? Pray with me that the seeds you have sown through your prayers will see fruition and be ready for harvest because of the mighty flowing river of God.

2. How can you invite your children to pray with you? How can you help them wait for the fruit of their prayers? How can you celebrate seasons of fruitfulness with your family?

154

Expectant Belief

Psalm 27:13-14 (Amplified Bible)

{What, what would have become of me} had I not believed that I would see the Lord's goodness in the land of the living! Wait and hope for and expect the Lord; be brave and of good courage and let your heart be stout and enduring. Yes, wait for and hope for and expect the Lord.

What would become of me if I did not believe? There are several levels of believing described here by the psalmist. The first foundational level is believing that God is good. Many people have a difficult time with this basic belief: believing that God is good, all the time, in every aspect. His goodness is His glory; it is part of His character and Person, and is something that can never be altered in any form. As challenging as this first tier belief can be, we are urged to believe further. The psalmist writes that he not only believes in God's goodness, but he also believes that he will see it! He personally will see, experience, and know the goodness of God. However, there is another level of belief! He believes that he will see the goodness of God in the land of the living! He has faith that he will see and experience God's goodness in this earthly life. What would have become of him had he believed that God's goodness was only for heaven, and not for today, for this life?

He then speaks about living with a posture of hope and expectation, and also bravery and good courage while waiting to see God's goodness. He waits with an enduring heart. He shares that this is how he lives. He lives with a belief, a faith, and a posture of expectation, even in waiting times. He invites us to do the same—to live with a posture of expectancy for good, for personal experiences with God, and for God's Kingdom to come to earth.

1. How would you describe your belief system about God, this life, and goodness?

2. How does your belief system affect your posture and expectation in prayer and in your daily life? Can you accept the psalmist's invitation to live with an elevated level of faith and expectation that God's goodness and glory will invade your household?

155

ASK GOD

JAMES 4:2 (NEW INTERNATIONAL VERSION)

You do not have because you do not ask God.

As a parent, I have asked God for many things that I have laid at His feet in prayer. However, when I read this verse, I wonder if there are things that I need or desire that I have not even asked for. Are there things, for example, that I don't believe God for and therefore don't ask for? Am I limiting my prayers before God in any way? For example, do I ask for the moon? Or, do I ask for things that I think are somehow most possible or realistic? Do I limit myself to things that I think are most holy or legitimate? I would hate to come before the very Presence of God and have Him ask me why I believed in Him for so little. I would hate for Him to say that there were things He longed to release in my life or the life of my child that were not released because I didn't ask and because I believed for too little. I would hate to find out that I'd been self-limiting and therefore had limited the power of God to move in my life.

I want to choose to believe God for abundant goodness. I want to believe Him for "too much," if that is possible, although I don't think it is, except in my own limited mind. I choose to ask for the moon, to pray for the impossible, to see a future in places where there seems to be a dead end in the now. I choose to keep asking for more and more goodness from a good God. I pray for more of Him: for more life, for more freedom, for more healing, and for no limits. I pray the same for you, your children, your marriage, and your household.

1. Is there any way that you are tempted to limit God or to limit your requests and prayers? If you were to "ask for the moon," what would that look like? Ask for it now!

2. I challenge you to honor and worship God by asking and believing for more of His goodness. I know He has more to give us. Let's ask together!

Made in the USA
Charleston, SC
03 October 2012